Drongo's

Guide to...

BBQ Mastery

Drongo's Guide to BBQ Mastery

by Ross Yarranton

Published by JoJo Publishing

'Yarra's Edge'
2203/80 Lorimer Street
Docklands VIC 3008
Australia

Email: jo-media@bigpond.net.au or visit www.jojopublishing.com

© 2007 JoJo Publishing

JoJo Publishing

Yarranton, Ross.
Drongo's guide to bbq mastery : a guide for the drongo in all of us.

ISBN 9 78098032 1678 (pbk.).

1. Barbecue cookery. 2. Cookery, Australian.
I. Title.

641.5784

Edited by Charlotte Strong
Illustrated by Roger Harvey
Designed by Modern Art Production Group
Printed in China by Everbest Printing Co. Ltd.

Drongo's

Guide to...

BBQ Mastery

by Ross Yarranton

Acknowledgments

This book is dedicated to my wife Hazel, who is and always will be my strongest and dearest food critic. May she continue to be so!

To my family and friends who have endured my barbeque cooking over the years with grateful encouragement – without them this book may not have made it to the bookshelves.

Finally to my editor Charlotte who has worked long and hard to get my scribble into some sort of order ready for print!

Thank you all.

Contents

Introduction

About the author

Ross Yarranton was born in London on September 9, 1952. After a less than successful school education, he went on to college and eventually began a career at Shell UK in London, following in his father's footsteps in marketing and oil. This stage of his career spanned about ten years, with Ross ending up at Shell's head office in The Strand, Central London.

In 1979 Ross moved to South London to work for his uncle in oil and gas at Star Fuels Oils Ltd, primarily in the LPG division, handling both butane and propane gases. This was where his interest in barbeques was born.

In 1989, having reached the heights of Sales and Marketing Director at the age of 35, Ross and his wife Hazel decided to emigrate to Australia to 'try something different'.

After trying his hand at a variety of different jobs, Ross decided that working for somebody else would never be in his career plan, and he set up his own home maintenance business in 1996.

The initial break for the start of this new business came during a barbeque party at his home, when he thought to himself, 'who assembles and maintains barbeques in Perth?' He visited the local barbeque store the following day and from that moment, his barbeque repair business was born.

Barbitec was formed in 2000 when barbeque servicing, repairs and manufacturers warranty work started to form the greater part of the business. During this time Ross developed an interest in cooking – mainly the evening meals for his hard-working wife! Ross found he was good at 'experimenting' with food dishes. This led to two years of recipe collaboration with professional chefs in Western Australia, and then the formation of the 'cooking' side of his business!

Ross then decided to combine simple barbeque maintenance techniques and cookery classes into one instructional class, which led to the idea of writing this book…The Drongo's Guide to BBQ Mastery!

Ross is married to Hazel and they have two adorable dogs. His sister lives in Sydney with her family and his mum, now in Perth, immigrated to Australia a few years ago when Ross's father Peter passed away.

Ross is a fully qualified and licensed gas technician.

'I hope that you will enjoy this book and use it to its full extent. It has been designed to take you through all the steps from buying, storing and maintaining your barbeque, to making the most of cooking on it! All the recipes and instructions are easy to follow... so enjoy and Bon Appetit!'

Ross

Why you need this book

There have been loads of cookbooks written over the past few years, including barbeque cookbooks, but how many times have you looked up a recipe and then realised that you don't have the ingredients, equipment or know-how to actually make it?

What this book offers is a step-by-step guide to every aspect of 'good old Aussie barbequing'. From buying your barbeque and accessories, to cooking up full barbeque menus to feed a crowd, this book literally takes you from start to finish. By following the easy-to-understand instructions, tips and guidelines, you will end up with deliciously simple food that tastes great and is good for you. Before you know it, you will have earned the reputation amongst your friends and family as 'the barbeque master'!

Sit back and read this book BEFORE you start cooking and use it page by page as you go. Don't worry if you get food and grease on it – your guests and friends will appreciate a great barbeque, great food and know you've had a great time using it!

Good luck and enjoy!

Conventions in this book

Icons

Underneath each recipe in this book you will find picture icons that tell you certain things about that particular recipe.

 This icon indicates how many people the recipe will feed. You may like to halve or double the recipe quantities depending on how many people you're cooking for.

 This icon indicates approximately how long it will take to prepare the ingredients before you start cooking.

 This icon indicates approximately how long it will take to cook the recipe.

 This icon indicates that you need a barbeque with a roasting hood to cook this particular recipe.

 This icon indicates that you need a barbeque with a side burner to cook this particular recipe. Some recipes with this icon may be cooked on the hotplate if you don't have a side burner. The recipe text will tell you whether this is the case. Alternatively, you can use your kitchen stove.

Cooking times

Cooking times can vary, depending on the type and size of your barbeque, the weather (windy and cold conditions may affect how you barbeque performs), and the type of fuel you use. The cooking times given in the recipes are approximate only, so it's a good idea to always keep an eye on what you're cooking and check it a few minutes before the recommended time is up, just in case it's already done.

Measurement conversions

1 cup	250 ml (9 fl oz)
1 teaspoon (tsp)	5 ml
1 tablespoon (tbsp)	20 ml

Explanations

Bake To cook under the roasting hood of the barbeque. Food is cooked slowly with gentle heat, causing the natural moisture to evaporate slowly, concentrating the flavour.

Baste To brush or spoon liquid fat or juices over meat during roasting to add flavor and to prevent it from drying out.

Blanch To boil briefly to loosen the skin of a fruit or a vegetable. After 30 seconds in boiling water, the fruit or vegetable should be plunged into ice water to stop the cooking action, and then the skin easily slices off.

Blend To mix or fold two or more ingredients together to obtain equal distribution throughout the mixture.

Boil To cook food in heated water (or other liquid) that is bubbling vigorously.

Braise A cooking technique that requires browning meat in oil or other fat and then cooking slowly in liquid. The effect of braising is to tenderise the meat.

Brown A quick sautéing, pan/oven broiling, or grilling method done either at the beginning or end of meal preparation, often to enhance flavour, texture, or visual appeal.

Butterfly To cut open a food such as pork chops down the center without cutting all the way through, and then spread apart.

Chop To cut into irregular pieces.

Coat To evenly cover food with flour, crumbs, or a batter.

Cure To preserve or add flavor with an ingredient, usually salt and/or sugar.

Dash A measure approximately equal to 1/16 teaspoon.

Deep-fry To completely submerge the food in hot oil.

Dice To cut into cubes.

Drippings Used for gravies and sauces, drippings are the liquids left in the bottom of a roasting or frying pan after meat is cooked.

Fillet To remove the bones from meat or fish for cooking.

Fry To cook food in hot cooking oil or on the barbeque hotplate, usually until a crisp brown crust forms.

Garnish A decorative piece of an edible ingredient such as parsley, lemon wedges, croutons, or chocolate curls placed as a finishing touch to dishes or drinks.

Grate To shred or cut down a food into fine pieces by rubbing it against a rough surface.

Grease To coat a pan or skillet with a thin layer of oil.

Grill To cook over the grill plate of the barbeque.

Jus The natural juices released by roasting meats.

Marinate To combine food with aromatic ingredients to add flavor.

Mash To beat or press a food to remove lumps and make a smooth mixture.

Medallion A small round or oval bit of meat.

Mince To chop food into tiny, irregular pieces. Also refers to meat such as beef or pork that has been ground into tiny pieces (beef mince, pork mince).

Pan-fry To cook in a hot pan with small amount of hot oil, butter, or other fat, turning the food over once or twice.

Pare To peel or trim a food, usually vegetables.

Pinch Same as 'dash'.

Poach To simmer in liquid.

Purée To mash or sieve food into a thick liquid.

Reconstitute To take a dried food such as milk back to its original state by adding liquid.

Reduce To cook liquids down so that some of the water evaporates.

Refresh To pour cold water over freshly cooked vegetables to prevent further cooking and to retain colour.

Roast To cook under the roasting hood of the barbeque.

Sauté To cook food quickly in a small amount of oil in a skillet or sauté pan over direct heat.

Score To tenderise meat by making a number of shallow (often diagonal) cuts across its surface. This technique is also useful in marinating, as it allows for better absorption of the marinade.

Sear Sealing in a meat's juices by cooking it quickly under very high heat.

Season To enhance the flavor of foods by adding ingredients such as salt, pepper and a variety of other herbs, spices, condiments, and vinegars.

Simmer Cooking food in a liquid at a low enough temperature that small bubbles begin to break the surface.

Skim To remove the top fat layer from stocks, soups, sauces, or other liquids such as cream from milk.

Steam To cook over boiling water in a covered pan, this method keeps foods' shape, texture, and nutritional value intact better than methods such as boiling.

Stew To brown small pieces of meat, poultry, or fish, then simmer them with vegetables or other ingredients in enough liquid to cover them, usually in a closed pot on the side burner (or stove) or under the roasting hood.

Stir-fry The fast frying of small pieces of meat and vegetables over very high heat with continual and rapid stirring.

Truss To use string, skewers, or pins to hold together a food to maintain its shape while it cooks (usually applied to meat or poultry).

Vinaigrette A general term referring to any sauce made with vinegar, oil, and seasonings.

Why the barbeque is best!

Barbequing has been the preferred method of cooking since caveman times! (Actually, cavemen didn't have much choice when it came to cooking methods, but with barbequing they were certainly on to a good thing!). These days, from 'throwing a shrimp on the barbie' on Australia Day, to preparing a gourmet barbeque feast for Christmas lunch, the use of barbeques for cooking has become an Australian lifestyle trademark, and one that we are all proud of.

The Australian climate and conditions are perfect for cooking outdoors, which is one of the reasons that barbequing is so popular in this country. There are other reasons too – barbequing is a healthy, easy way to cook, and it can be a great social event. There's nothing more relaxing and enjoyable than having a drink or two with friends, while you stand around in the sun, watching steaks and sausages sizzle!

The reason why barbequing is considered healthy is because once you've oiled up your barbeque hotplates and grills, not a lot of extra oils or fats are needed. Unlike some traditional indoor cooking methods, the barbeque allows you to flavour your food with herbs and spices, instead of relying heavily on oil. As well as this, fresh healthy salads and vegetables are a traditional accompaniment to barbequed food.

Apart from the health and social benefits of barbequing, there's one other little benefit that everyone will appreciate – compared to cooking indoors, there's a lot less cleaning up involved!

1

A Basic Introduction to the Barbeque

Barbeque diagram

This diagram shows a modern barbeque with all the bells and whistles. When purchasing a barbeque, you may choose one with some or all of these features. Either way, it's important to understand what each part of your barbeque is used for and how to look after it properly so that you get the best out of your barbeque! (See Chapters 1, 3 and 4.)

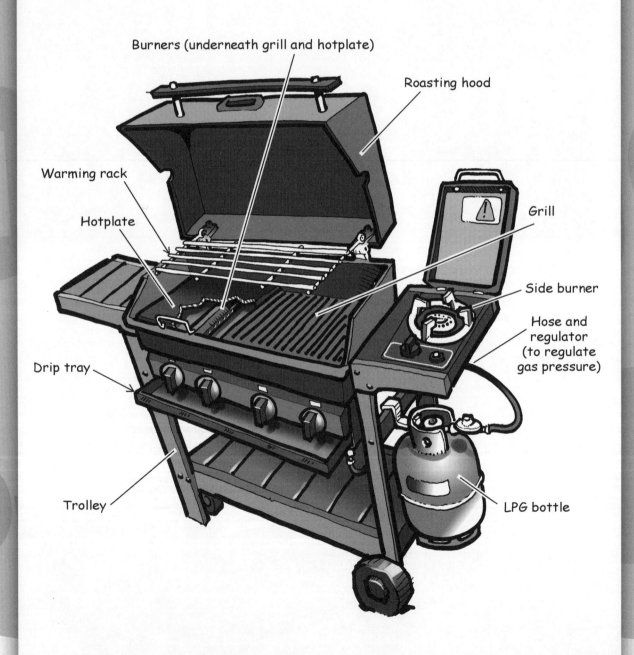

Burners (underneath grill and hotplate)

Roasting hood

Warming rack

Hotplate

Grill

Side burner

Hose and regulator (to regulate gas pressure)

Drip tray

Trolley

LPG bottle

Which type of barbeque?

There are many different types and brands of barbeques on the market and all of them promise to be the best. When you are looking to buy a new barbeque, regardless of brand, there are a few things you need to do:

1. Do your research.
    Good news! If you are reading this, then you are already doing your research!

2. Decide how sophisticated you want your barbeque to be.

   The best way to do this is to estimate how many people you will regularly be cooking for, and what types of dishes you'll be making. For example, if you are only cooking for 2–4 people, and are unlikely to cook anything more complicated than sausages and steaks, a flat top barbeque will be enough to get you by. However, if your cooking expectations are a little higher, and/or you expect that you'll sometimes be cooking for more people, then you'll need a barbeque with at least two burners and a hood. The table on page 5 will help you choose the type of barbeque that is right for you.

Tip: A hooded barbeque basically turns the outdoor barbeque into an all-in-one cooking machine, complete with oven. It can have 1, 2, 3, 4, 5, or 6 or more burners plus a wok or side burner and an infra-red grill or rotisserie. You can use a barbeque without a hood but any roasts will have to be cooked inside in a conventional oven. Everything else can normally be cooked on the barbeque!

Hotplates, grills & burners

Cast iron vs. stainless steel

Traditionally, cast iron hotplates, grills and burners have been used in most barbeques, but these days stainless steel is becoming a more popular alternative.

Cast iron:

When bought new, cast iron hotplates and grills usually have a clear coating to help prevent them from rusting in transit from the manufacturer. This coating is harmless and disappears when the hotplate is 'cured', but to keep the hotplates from rusting and flaking in the future, they must be oiled. Cast iron is a porous metal that easily retains the flavour of food. Because of this, a really good clean after cooking is essential. Cast iron is cheaper than stainless steel and can be broken or chipped. It can come in all thicknesses and can be enamel coated for more protection. As cast iron hotplates are normally black in colour, you tend not to see any burn or food marks on the surface.

Stainless steel:

Stainless steel hotplates are rust-resistant, corrosion-resistant and non-porous. They retain heat for longer and no 'curing' is necessary. They will last a lifetime (if looked after properly!) and will not absorb flavours. However, they are considerably more expensive than cast iron.

One manufacturer, Topnotch, sells a hotplate that is coated in Exlan (a superior non-stick coating, similar to Teflon). These hotplates come in various sizes to suit most barbeques, and can be cleaned simply by wiping down with paper towels. They are a worthwhile investment for the discerning barbeque chef.

Stainless steel is light in colour so you do see what you have cooked on it, and the hotplates will permanently discolour if olive oil is placed directly onto them when they are hot (see Chapter 3 for which oils to use on your barbeque). The same thing happens to cast iron, but as the surface is black you won't notice it as much.

Hoods, burners, grills, hotplates and trolleys now all come in stainless steel. As stainless steel is more expensive, it is important to keep it clean so that it lasts longer. See Chapter 4 for advice on keeping your hotplates and grills clean and free from bugs!

Author's tip: At the end of the day no matter which barbeque you choose, it will only be as good as the condition in which you keep it – so be kind to your barbeque! Clean it regularly and cover it when not in use, and you will be repaid with endless good times and delicious meals!

Which barbeque is right for me?

Barbeque type	Portability + fuel type	Size	Price range and lastability	Suits
Weber/ Kettle-style BBQ (with lid) **(Usually enamel coated)**	Light and portable Available in small and large sizes Fuel options include charcoal, briquettes and gas	Small and convenient, can usually cook for 2–6 people max	$299 to $400+ Should last 3–10 years	A couple, or a very small family wanting to mostly open-grill their food People with price restrictions who still want the flexibility of a hooded barbeque
Flat top BBQ, 4 burners **(Painted or enamel coated)**	Semi-portable Gas portability depends on gas type	Medium, can usually cook for 4–8 people max	$200 to $400 Should last 2–5 years	Anyone wanting a basic barbeque that is big enough to cook for friends and family but without all the bells and whistles Anyone who wants a basic but useful barbeque in the low to medium price range Would suit colleges, schools and sporting clubs
Hooded BBQ, 4–6 burners **(Enamel coated and partly stainless steel)**	Semi-portable Gas portability depends on gas type	Large, can usually cook for 8–12 people	$500 to $1500+ Should last 5–10 years	Anyone wanting to cook a variety of interesting recipes, including roasts, for a small or large group of people Anyone who uses their barbeque as a substitute for a kitchen
Hooded BBQ, 4–6 burners, with side or wok burner and infra-red grill for rotisserie cooking **(Enamel coated and partly or fully stainless steel)**	Semi-portable Gas portability depends on gas type	Large, can usually cook for 8–12 people	$1500 to $6000+ Should last 10+ years	For the discerning cook/chef wanting to cook a variety of interesting recipes, including roasts and dishes normally made on the stovetop, and in use at least two to three times a week for a small or large group of people

Note: Lastability is a general term given for a barbeque's life – this will depend on how the barbeque is looked after and how regularly it's cleaned and serviced!

Ignition systems

The knobs on the front of the barbeque are used to supply gas to the burners. They are usually turned anti-clockwise. When you turn the knob, it turns on the gas cock, which allows the gas to flow through a small hole (which is called an injector, or 'jet' for short) to the burners. The knob can be turned to adjust the gas flow from high to medium to low.

Some gas cocks also double up as ignitions, A flame thrower is a gas cock, which, when you turn the knob attached to it, throws a flame across the left or right-hand side of the burner to light it. When you release the knob after you hear it click, it leaves the gas on to light the burner. This is called a flame thrower ignition.

There are other types of ignition systems for barbeques. One such type is a Piezo ignition system. This works by the pressing of a button, which then sparks and lights the gas or electronic ignitions. These ignitions are are normally battery operated.

Most barbeques, with the exception of some flat top barbeques, have automatic ignition systems. If the automatic system fails then the barbeque can usually be lit manually.

Using gas

There are two different types of gas you can use for your barbeque: LPG (bottle gas) and natural gas (mains gas)

Bottled gas

Pros

◎ Uses mostly propane (propane is a hotter and higher pressured gas, requiring smaller pipes to run through and can fuel a bigger barbeque more efficiently as there is little or no drop in gas pressure).

◎ It's portable and therefore convenient if you need to move the barbeque around.

◎ It's hotter than mains gas.

◎ You pay for it before you use it.

Cons

◎ You may run out in the middle of cooking so you need a spare bottle.

◎ As it's a higher pressured gas, it requires more careful handling and storing.

Mains gas

Pros

◎ It's convenient if your barbeque always stays in the same spot.

◎ It won't run out halfway through cooking.

◎ It's cheaper than bottled gas.

Cons

◎ It may be costly to install a connection.

◎ It's a permanent fitting so you cannot move your barbeque around.

◎ It's not as hot as bottled gas.

Author's tip: Pipe sizing is critical when using mains gas. You need a bigger volume of gas as it is lower pressured than propane, so make sure your gas technician gets the right pipe size for your barbeque's output… otherwise it may not be hot enough to cook on!

Converting gas types

Most barbeques are manufactured to run on LPG, although the more expensive models can sometimes be manufactured to run on mains gas as well.

Not all barbeques can be converted and not all conversion kits will fit all barbeques. So remember, if you want a barbeque to run off the mains, check before you buy that it can be converted and that either a kit is available from the manufacturer or it can be built at the factory to your mains gas specifications.

The conversion process is complicated and should only be carried out by a qualified, licensed and experienced tradesperson. Should your barbeque still be under its warranty period, it is recommended that you use the manufacturer's authorised service agent. That way, you can be sure that the conversion will be done correctly and the warranty on your barbeque will remain valid.

Other fuels

There are other fuels that can be used instead of gas.

Electricity

Electric barbeques are plugged into an electrical power socket. These types of barbeques are usually small and pretty basic, but useful in confined areas.

Charcoal or briquettes

Charcoal or briquette barbeques were widely used before gas barbeques were commercially available. Charcoal or briquettes can be used in a standard Webber or kettle-style barbeque with a dome shaped lid. The advantage of using these fuels is that you usually get a better flavour than if you use gas or electricity, and the barbeque usually heats up fairly quickly. The disadvantage of using these fuels is they cannot be used on total fire ban days. Also, as the coals burn up you lose temperature, meaning that food will take longer to cook. However, a hot temperature at the beginning and cooler temperature at the end is particularly good for cooking large roasts.

Building and using an alfresco area

Alfresco means 'in the fresh air' or 'outdoors'. In Australia, the warm climate allows alfresco dining areas to be very much a part of the outdoor life. These areas can be used at any time of the year – winter or summer, day or night! They are generally built as indoor/outdoor areas – sheltered from the rain and sun but open enough to be considered part of 'the outdoors'.

You may decide you want to build an alfresco area with a barbeque for entertaining. However, be aware that not all states have the same laws for using gas appliances, so you will need to check with your local gas supplier before you install or use a gas appliance in a semi-enclosed area. Also keep in mind that not all types of barbeques are appropriate for semi-enclosed areas.

Go through the checklist below BEFORE you spend any money building an alfresco area!

Building/planning checklist

1. Check with your local gas supplier and energy safety department (or the equivalent government energy authority in your state) about regulations for using gas cooking facilities in a semi-enclosed area.

2. Check with your builder that he has got the relevant gas authority to check your area to ensure you can put a barbeque in it.

3. If you already own a barbeque, check that it is appropriate to use in semi-indoor areas.

4. Plan to install a proper extractor fan – this is a non-negotiable necessity. Commercial quality fans are usually required. This is a specialist area and should be handled by an expert.

5. Finally, check with your local, licensed and qualified gas technician/installer that the area you plan to build is suitable for a barbeque that is normally used outdoors.

Location and landscaping around the barbeque

If you decide against building a dedicated 'alfresco area' but still want your barbeque to have a place in the backyard, it's important to prepare your space properly. Here are a few tips:

◎ Keep the space clear of plants that might catch on fire. (Fire resistant plants include Agapanthus, Coprosma, Ficus, Ligustrum, Pelargonium, Populus (Poplar) and most cacti or succulents.)

◎ Build a wall or fence (preferably fire resistant), nearby to protect the barbeque from wind.

◎ Keep a table or bench near the barbeque to place raw and cooked food on.

◎ Outdoor tables and chairs should be far away enough from the barbeque to avoid any problems with smoke or spitting fats.

◎ Install lighting so that you can see what you're doing when cooking at night-time.

◎ Consider the surface underneath your barbeque. Gravel is the best surface to use because it won't develop ugly permanent stains from oils and fats. Concrete and sandstone are some of the worst materials for staining.

2

Essential Safety Information

You may feel inclined to skip over this chapter and wait until the common fat fire occurs before you refer back to it! But on a serious note, when you're dealing with gas, flames and heat, safety is very important and should be fully understood.

General safety - LPG

Standard gas bottle instructions state that each time you replace your LPG bottle, you should check for gas leaks with soapy water on the joint connections. This is important for safety and care, so try and make a habit of doing it! See the instructions on the next page.

General safety - mains gas

If you are not going to be using your barbeque for awhile, turn the isolation valve off or disconnect the gas supply at the bayonet.

How to check for gas leaks

Note: This is for flexible connections only. If your barbeque is connected to the gas supply by copper pipe, your gas fitter should have already done a leak test. If however, you do smell gas at any time when the barbeque is switched off, contact your local gas supplier or gas plumber as soon as possible.

Testing for leaks should be done regularly (about every 3 months for mains gas or whenever you change your gas bottle). It doesn't take long and is easy to do.

1. Half-fill a small glass with tap water and add a squeeze of dishwashing liquid. Take a small paint brush (one that will fit into the glass) and plunge it in a few times to create some suds.

2. Turn on the barbeque gas (either at the bottle or if on mains gas, by the bayonet connection). Do NOT turn on any of the burners!

3. Locate the gas regulator (the big metal thing that connects the hose to the bottle, or about halfway up the hose if on mains gas).

4. Brush some of the soapy solution on to where the gas regulator connects to the bottle, or on both sides of the regulator if on a flexible bayonet connection.

5. Follow the hose up to the barbeque. Brush some solution over the brass fitting/s that connect the hose to the barbeque and/or side burner.

6. If you see any soapy bubbles getting bigger, this indicates that there is a leak.

7. If a leak is detected, use a spanner to tighten up the connections, but don't over-tighten! If you still see bubbles forming after tightening the connections, turn off the valve at the bottle or remove the bayonet connection and contact your barbeque or gas supplier. They will advise the next course of action you should take.

Fat fires

Preventing fat fires

Most barbeque fires are caused by excess use of oil and fat, or a build up of fat, or both.

Take note of how much fat is in the food you are preparing to cook. Sausages are a prime example – they have a high content of fat and water (but are nowhere as bad as what they used to be!). Needless to say, sausages DO NOT need any fat to accompany them when cooking on a barbeque. Chipolata sausages are a good alternative to regular snags, as they are a convenient size for a snack or nibbles and they also contain a lot less fat than conventional larger sausages. Don't be afraid to ask your butcher how much meat compared to fat is in your chipolatas – if they are low in fat then they may be a bit more expensive, but they won't burn as much and they won't take as long to cook (and they are better for you!).

Instead of cooking sausages or chipolatas on the hotplates or grills, try using the 'warming rack' when heating up the barbeque with the hood down. This way they tend to be less susceptible to 'flaring' (and will be crispier than when cooked on the grill or hotplate!).

Always check the drip tray for excessive build-up of fat after each barbeque. If there is excessive build-up, you will need to clean out the drip tray (see cleaning instructions on page 32).

How to put out a fat fire

Fat fires are caused by using too much oil, or by or a build-up of fat on the drip tray or hotplates after several barbeques, or both.

If you have a fat fire, try not to panic, and remember to NEVER use water to put out the flames! Here is the correct way to put out a fat fire:

If the barbeque hood is down:

Turn off the gas bottle or gas valve. Do not open the hood! If you do then the fire will get air and the flames will be aggravated. Simply wait for the gas to stop flowing through the hose and the flames will soon subside.

If the barbeque hood is up:

Turn off the gas and use a damp towel to smother the flames. Then walk away and let the barbeque cool down.

> Do not attempt to put out the fire if it's out of control – in that case, call the fire brigade.

General barbeque safety tips

◎ Stand back from the barbeque and use long-handled implements to turn the food.

◎ As soon as you have finished cooking, turn off the burners and then turn off the gas at the bottle or gas connection. Try and make this process a habit!

◎ Don't touch the food with your hands while it is still on the barbeque! Apart from being unhygienic, it's also a great way to get painful finger burns!

◎ The old saying 'too many cooks in the kitchen' can literally mean disaster when it comes to using barbeques. Don't let groups of people huddle over the barbeque whilst cooking – make sure that you have plenty of space around you to move freely.

◎ Use oven mitts or tea towels to move pots or griller hotplates around.

3

Tools of the Trade

Barbeque accessories

It's important to have the right accessories for barbeque cooking – they'll make barbequing easier and enable you to cook your food to perfection! Having the right tools also means you'll avoid ruining your kitchen utensils (the heat that a barbeque puts out is very intense and can destroy the types of pots and pans that you would use for cooking in your kitchen).

Most of the accessories that you need are designed specifically for barbeque cooking and are available from your local barbeque shop, and sometimes from hardware stores. They are thicker and more durable than regular kitchenware and will last a long time if used and looked after properly. These accessories are usually relatively inexpensive for the quality that they are.

The list can be endless, but let's just start with a few basics:

Tongs:

Make sure you use good-quality, sturdy barbeque tongs. These are longer and thicker than regular tongs and make turning food over on a high heat so much easier.

Spatula:

These are fairly robust and aren't as flexible as the ones you would normally use in the kitchen, but are great for scraping down hotplates and grills and for moving food, especially meat and fish, straight from the barbeque on to the serving tray.

Fisharoo:

This comes in very handy when cooking fish or seafood of any type, including whole fish. A fisharoo works on the same principle as a normal roasting rack, but holds the fish in place. Due to its design it raises the fish like a meat rack does to achieve more 'even cooking' and prevent sticking. You can cook any seafood in it – even prawns and scallops!

Smoker box:

Using a smoker box is the ideal way to create that delicious smoky flavour in meat or fish. A smoker box comes with wooden chips that help to create the flavour, and various flavoured chips, such as apple and hickory, are available. There are two ways to use the wooden chips:

Soak the chips in water for about ten minutes, then place them in the box.

OR

Place the chips in the smoker box and sprinkle some water on them.

The second method will produce a more intense smoky flavour, but increases the chances of the chips catching alight during the cooking process.

There are also two ways to cook with the smoker box:

Place the box on the grill

OR

Place the box directly on the burner below the grill

Again, the second method will intensify the flavour. So, if you want that ultra-intense smoked flavour and you're willing to risk it catching alight, sprinkle the wooden chips with water, throw in your meat or fish, and place the box directly on the barbeque burner!

Warming rack:

This is an essential accessory for any barbeque. If you haven't already got one of these go out and buy one now! You can get chrome or enamel – both are good, but the enamel is easier to keep clean.

The warming rack is not necessarily just for warming the food or keeping it warm, as placing cooked food on this rack can sometimes dry it out, so we can also refer to it as a cooking rack.

The warming/cooking rack is:

◎ Great for cooking other food while the barbeque is heating up for roasts (i.e. you don't waste that heat and energy waiting for the barbeque to warm up).

◎ Great for cooking sausages! You can put sausages onto the rack, straight from the freezer, with no extra fat.

◎ Very versatile! The versatility of the rack is terrific as it provides additional room for cooking and allows food to cook with an all-round heat, as it is raised up and has continual heat convection.

Meat thermometer:

Chefs are experienced professionals and always know (well almost always!) when meat is cooked, just by looking at it. Don't forget that they cook all the time and that instinctively knowing when food is ready is their specialist skill! You can cheat however by using a meat thermometer. These handy little tools are not expensive and are a definite must for the barbeque cook – especially if you're aiming to impress your guests! Try to get one that shows both the temperatures and the type of meat to cook beside the temperatures. It makes it a lot easier to tell when a particular type of meat is cooked. Always take your meat off the heat one notch before the desired temperature is reached, as your meat will continue to cook whilst 'resting'.

Baking dish and rack:

Baking racks vary in size and type, but the most versatile is probably the 'V' shaped one, mainly because it can fit a normal small baking dish and also because it is designed to 'overlap' the dish, so it can hold a piece of meat that is larger than the dish below it.

  Racks are another essential barbeque accessory, as they raise the meat up while it's cooking to get an even amount of heat around the food and to prevent the meat stewing in its own juices. As it's raised you can add stock, wine, herbs etc. in the final phase, to give the meat flavour and to prevent it from drying out.

Wok:

In recent years the popularity of Asian cooking has exploded in Australia, so it's no surprise that we can now create healthy, delicious Asian-inspired dishes on our barbeques! Many Asian dishes, especially stir-fries, require the use of a 'wok'. Unfortunately wok burners on barbeques are hard to find, unless you buy an expensive up-market barbeque. However, most barbeques on the market these days at least have a side burner. These are quite different from wok burners (see below for a description of each) but can be used as a substitute – in fact, it's really no different from using a wok on your regular kitchen stove.

Definition of a side burner

A side burner is simply that – a burner that is attached to the side of your barbeque. It has only one burning ring that has a reasonably uniform flame that can be adjusted to low or high as desired. It is similar to a single hotplate burner that you would have in your kitchen, but put on the side of the barbeque for the use of a frying pan, saucepan or wok.

Definition of a wok burner

A wok burner has several rings of flame that supply heat to the entire base of the wok. This means that the wok gets hot very fast – perfect for Asian cooking, which is usually done very quickly over a very high temperature.

  Hopefully, as Asian cooking continues to grow in popularity, barbeque manufacturers will incorporate both a wok burner and a side burner into standard barbeque designs so that consumers have a choice.

Essential ingredients

Having a well set-up barbeque kitchen means that you'll never find yourself without that 'essential ingredient'. Nearly everything you need you'll probably already have at home, but if you're going to be using your barbeque regularly it's worth putting aside your barbeque ingredients in a separate kitchen space, and only use them when you use your barbeque! This way you'll always know that you're stocked up with what you need, and you'll never go to reach for something and find that someone else has put it elsewhere! It's all part of having the complete barbeque kit!

Here is what you'll need:

Oil

Oils with a high smoke or burn point are best for using on barbeques as there is less chance of burning your food. Good types to use include canola and sunflower oils. Canola oil will cook your food before it burns it, if used correctly. It is also excellent for keeping hotplates, grills and burners lubricated and helps prevent them from rusting.

Oils with a low smoke point produce a heavier smoke when cooked, and are therefore not recommended for using over high heat. These oils, which include olive, sesame, peanut and macadamia oils, are best to use for marinating and on salads. It's worth investing in a good olive oil – expect to pay about $30 a bottle – but the difference in flavour absolutely justifies the price, and you only need to use a small amount each time. Just don't waste it on oiling your barbeque!

Author's tip: You don't need to use a lot of oil on your hotplates and grills – just enough to keep them lubricated. A canola oil spray is a great option as you can't over-pour it and it lasts a long time.

Salt and Pepper

It's worth splashing out a bit and buying peppercorns and rock salt – once grounded, they taste better and are easier to use than the pre-packaged kind.

Herbs and Spices

The choices are endless when it comes to herbs and spices, but there are a few staples that you should always have on hand. These include basil, oregano, parsley, rosemary, thyme, coriander and of course, garlic. You can use dried or fresh herbs, but remember, fresh is always best!

Author's tip: If using fresh herbs, warm them under a running hot tap and then chop – this will boost their aroma and flavour.

Other basic ingredients

Fresh lemons – both the juice and the zest are great for marinating meat and dressing salads.

Onions – a classic on the barbeque.

Potatoes – another classic. Just slice and fry!

Food preparation and storage

You probably will have heard the word 'prep' from a Chef somewhere.

This of course means food preparation, i.e. preparing the food for cooking or storing or presenting.

This, apart from choosing and buying your food, is the most important part of barbequing.

We touched on buying food a bit earlier. This is an important topic and is just as important as keeping your barbeque in tip-top condition. After all, you wouldn't want to put cheap furniture in an expensive house so why put cheap meat on your barbeque?

Marinades

The most important thing to remember when buying marinated meat to cook on the barbeque is that light marinades enhance the flavour of food. Heavy marinades disguise it. Also be aware that heavy marinades may mean that the meat is a bit old or tired or a bad cut – this is not always the case, but if you're not sure then don't buy it!

Marinades also have citrus acids, sugar, vinegar and salt in them. Hotplates, grills and burners that are made of cast iron hate marinades as they can rust through the hotplates over time as they eat into the metal. One way to avoid this is to oil the hotplates, grills and burners every so often so that these juices won't stick to the cast iron.

Always buy fresh meat, as it will need hardly any oil or marinade, will cook well, shrink less and will tastes better.

> **Author tip:** Your guests will appreciate a little good quality food rather than a lot of food that is so tough that they can't eat it!

Storing food

Whenever you buy any food other than tinned or frozen, always consider whether you intend to eat it straight away or keep it for a few days. If it's a meat product ask your local butcher how long it can keep for, and if it's a deli item then ask your local delicatessen.

Some butchers can now vacuum pack meat while you wait. This greatly increases the storage time and in some cases can actually mature a roast blade or topside to make it more tender in the long term (if kept in a cold fridge). If you do have a piece of meat that won't last long, cook it then freeze it, rather than throwing it away.

Fresh food will obviously last a lot longer than stale food, and most fridges these days are designed to have a lower temperature setting to allow food to keep for longer. Some kitchenware can also improve storing times. For example, storing lettuce in a good quality salad spinner in a low temperature fridge may allow it to stay fresh for up to a week.

How to Look After Your Barbeque

Covers

Covers play an important part in preserving the life of a barbeque. There are four types you can purchase. Most are tailor-made for a particular barbeque model (so make sure you get the right one!) and some even come with the purchase of your barbeque.

A dust cover – made of flimsy flexible plastic, this cover offers minimum protection. It's good for keeping the dust off the barbeque while it's stored away in the shed. It's not suitable for outdoor use as the material is very easy to tear.

A shower-proof cover – made of soft vinyl, this cover is suitable for partially protecting your barbeque in semi-exposed areas like patios.

A waterproof cover – made of heavy duty rubber-type vinyl, this cover is quite strong and will protect your barbeque when it's out in the elements (i.e. outside in the garden).

A cover for built-in barbeques – made of soft vinyl, this cover generally offers shower-proof protection, although more waterproof styles are becoming available. This cover has an elastic edge that wraps around and tucks in under the barbeque, covering almost all of it (similar to a fitted sheet).

A cheap cover is better than none at all, but if you do have the money, it's worth investing in a good quality barbeque cover. It will really stand the test of time and will ensure that your barbeque does too!

If you do use a cover of any sort, don't leave it on the barbeque for prolonged periods of time. Some of the covers available these days are extremely effective and don't let a lot of air in to ventilate the barbeque, so when your barbeque is sitting on paving or a concrete surface and it rains, the moisture on the paving rises and causes condensation under the cover (especially when it's sunny after a shower or two). This can cause hotplates and trolleys to rust. So, every now and again, take the cover off to let your barbeque breathe!

Burners

It's important to know how burners work so that you have an understanding of what may go wrong with them if they're not looked after properly!

The burners are the engines of your barbeque, so keeping them clean is a must if you want your barbeque to work efficiently. It's a bit like checking the oil in your car.

Keeping the burners in good condition is very easy. Take out the hotplates and grills and the flame tamers or rock tray, and underneath you will see the burners. Depending on the size of the barbeque, you may have 2, 4 or 6 burners. Most burners are easy to get out as they lift up from the back and pull from the front. Some have screws on the top at the back or clips underneath so check this before you pull them out.

On inspection the burners should be clean and in good condition. If they're not, use a wire brush to remove the flaky rust and make sure the ports (the hole on either side) are clear and unblocked. Then put the burners back into the barbeque. Do not 'hose them down' as this will increase the chance of rust forming.

> **Author's tip:** Every now and again, swap the burners between the grill and hotplate and they will last longer.

When the burners have been put back, spray them with canola oil (canola is best – as mentioned earlier it has a high smoke and burn point). Only use a light spray but make sure you cover them well.

If your barbeque has a fitted cast iron flame tamer, spray it with canola oil. Also spray the grill and hotplates, then put everything back together. The barbeque is now ready for use.

This exercise should be done at the start of each summer. Cast iron barbeque burners cost approximately $20 each to replace so it's worth keeping them well maintained.

Drip tray

The drip tray (also referred to as the fat tray) is an integral part of the barbeque and has several purposes. It collects fats and marinades from the hotplates and grills. It also protects the burners from wind, protects the barbeque trolley (if fitted) from excessive heat, and helps to keep the heat 'in'.

A lot of people still use ordinary yellow sand in the bottom of their drip tray. Although sand is cheap, it is not recommended for the following reason… sand, by nature, does not absorb fats fully and when heated causes the fats to adhere to the sand like glue. It is then very hard to clean off, especially if the fats build up in the sand over time.

There is a product that is made especially for use in drip trays, called Fat Soak. It is highly absorbent, has no fragrance and is normally white in colour. Fat Soak should be changed at least twice a year and will go brown when ready to change, which is a handy reminder! Don't leave it in the tray for too long as it will become hard to remove and can attract insects.

When you need to replace the granules do the following:

For drip trays without a hole in the middle:

Take the drip tray out and remove whatever is in it. Use a wire brush to scrape off any fats and oils that are stuck to the tray's surface. Clean the tray with soap and water and dry thoroughly.

Spray the drip tray liberally with canola oil (or similar) and place one layer of foil neatly in the tray, ensuring that the edges of the foil do not overlap the tray. (The oil prevents the foil from lifting and makes it easier to remove when replacing.)

If you need to put another layer of foil in the tray, spray the foil that's already in the tray and place the second layer of foil on top.

Pour the new granules into the tray and spread evenly. You may need at least two bags, as it's important to get about a 10 mm thickness. If it's any spread any thinner then this it won't do its job!

Pick up the whole tray and place it back into the barbeque.

For drip trays with a hole in the middle:

Follow the directions above. After placing the foil in the tray, make a small hole in the middle of the foil and place the granules in the little tray below the hole. Do NOT place the granules in the tray itself.

Curing the hotplates and grills

If you have stainless steel hotplates and grills no curing is required, but any cast iron cooking surface has to be cured (or seasoned) before use. This is to get rid of the factory coating and to give the hotplate a semi non-stick surface. Curing hotplates and grills is actually very easy.

You will need some paper towels, canola oil spray, some water in a bucket and a barbeque scrub brush.

First spray the hotplates and grills lightly with canola oil. Next, light the barbeque and put all the burners on to the high setting until you can see smoke coming from the hotplates (about 2–3 minutes should be enough time). Then, turn the burners down to the lowest setting, dip the scrub brush in the bucket of water and scrub the hotplates and grills lightly and continuously, dipping into the water every so often to keep the brush lubricated. After 2–3 minutes of scrubbing, turn the burners off. The water will then dry off and you should then coat the hotplates and grills lightly again with canola oil before the first use.

It's a good idea to regularly spray the hotplates and grills with canola oil. This will help prevent them from rusting, and it also enables some of the juices and acids from the food to fall off the grills more easily when cooking.

The barbeque burners should also be coated with canola oil prior to use as this protects the cast iron and allows the food juices to roll off the burners, onto the drip tray below.

Cleaning and storing

This is the bit we all like, isn't it! Cleaning your barbeque is not hard to do if it's done when the barbeque is still hot.

For cast iron hotplates and grills use the following cleaning method:

If it's just oil that's on the hotplates and grills, use a barbeque scraper to remove excess food and then use newspaper or paper towels to wipe off any excess fat or grease. To finish, spray lightly with canola oil.

If your hotplates and grills are badly soiled then follow the instruction above, but after scraping off the excess food, use a scrubber brush (available from most barbeque outlets) and a half bucket of water and with the barbeque burners turned on low, scrub the hotplates and grills continuously until most of the grime is removed. Don't press too hard on the hotplates and grills.

Next, turn the burners off and clean the hotplates and grills with paper, and finish up with a light spray of canola oil.

For stainless steel hotplates and grills use the following cleaning method:

Cleaning stainless steel hotplates (other than the non-stick type) is a little bit different. You will need a scrubber brush and a cleaning mixture of 50% vinegar and 50% water.

With the burners turned on, pour a little of the mix onto the hotplates and scrub lightly. Continue until most of the fat and oil has gone, then dip the scrubber in the mix and do the same with the grills.

Clean with paper and spray with canola oil.

To clean the warming rack, remove the rack and clean it with a scouring pad or scrubber.

Cleaning the roasting hood is a little bit more difficult. If it's only lightly soiled, a spray with a barbeque cleaner designed for hoods will suffice, but if it's well soiled, an oven spray needs to be used. Be careful to follow the manufacturer's instructions as some hoods have aluminium in them and as most oven cleaners are caustic this can discolour the metals.

When cooking on a barbeque, a special Teflon sheet that sits directly over the hotplate can be used. Using a Teflon sheet is worth considering if you really don't want to spend time cleaning your barbeque, or if you want to extend the life of your hotplates and grills. These Teflon sheets are sold at most barbeque retailers, and if your local barbeque store doesn't have them in stock they should be able to order them in for you. To use this Teflon sheet, place it onto the hotplate, and cook on it as you would on a cast iron or stainless steel surface. Remember though to use a plastic spatula or tongs, otherwise you will rip the sheet. After use it can be washed under a tap and wiped. These sheets are great for cooking fish and sticky food such as fruit.

5

Ready to Start!

Checklist

This checklist will help you to get organised before you start cooking on your barbeque. It is especially helpful if you are cooking for a crowd!

◎ Is your barbeque clean, cured and ready to use?

◎ Are all your barbeque tools and accessories clean and ready to use?

◎ Have you re-filled the gas bottle?

◎ Do you know how many people you're cooking for?

◎ Are you stocked up with all the ingredients you'll need?

◎ Have you pre-marinated your meat?

◎ Do you have food options for the vegetarians among your guests?

◎ Do you have the right oils, spices and marinades on hand?

◎ Have you organised plates, cutlery, napkins etc. for your guests?

Warming up the barbeque for use

Warming up the barbeque is very important. Most barbeques these days have smaller burners or jets to prevent over-cooking or burning, so it's important to leave the burners on for long enough so that the hotplates and grills heat up to the right temperature, and the hood gets hot enough to cook a roast (if that's what you're cooking).

When heating up the hood, use the hood temperature gauge as an indicator but keep in mind that it's not completely accurate.

It takes about 10–20 minutes for most hotplates to heat up when used either with or without a hood, depending on the barbeque.

How to tell when it's hot enough

A good test is to put a tablespoon of water on the rear of the hotplate, as that's the hottest part on most barbeques. If the water disperses in all directions into tiny little beads then it's hot enough to use. If it stews in one place then you need to let it heat up for longer. Cold food placed onto the hotplate will cool it down quite rapidly, so it is essential to get the hotplate up to 'beading temperature' (this is referred to throughout this book).

Heat distribution

As mentioned earlier, the hottest part of most barbeques is at the rear. This is because the burners are designed to light on both sides and in order to do this the flame on one side travels under the burner to light the other side. This adds to the heat and reflects off the rear 'firewall' of the barbeque, which is why most barbeques are hotter at the back.

The coldest part of the barbeque is at the front. This is because in most barbeques, before the barbeque itself is lit, the gas and air mix together at the front and then travel along a small tube to the burner, which is located in the middle of the barbeque. No heat is generated until the burners are lit; therefore it is usually cooler towards the front.

Both of these areas and the one in the middle can be utilised in cooking food evenly. If you want to cook fast then use the back. If you want to cook slowly then use the front. If one of your food items is cooking faster than the rest, then move it to the front to slow the cooking process down. With a little practise, you will be able to cook so that all your dishes are ready to be served at the same time!

6

Popular Barbeque Dishes

Recipes in this chapter

A note about sealing: Most meat (with the exception of some chicken) requires sealing before cooking. If it's sealed before it's grilled it will retain the juices. If you put the meat straight onto the grill without sealing it completely, only the parts that the grill touches will be sealed and 50% of the juices will just fall straight through onto the flame tamers. If this happens you'll end up with dry, tough meat!

Steak (scotch fillet)

Scotch fillet is ideal for cooking on the barbeque for several reasons. It comes with lovely marbled fat in the meat which dissolves when cooked, making the meat moist and tender. Also, it doesn't take long to cook, and tastes fantastic!

Heat the hotplate and grills on high for 10–15 minutes. Do the beading test with water and when the hotplate and grills are hot enough, rub or spray some oil onto them (if they're not already oiled). When the hotplate starts to smoke, place the oil-brushed steaks onto it and cook for 45 seconds only, then transfer to the grill the same side up (this is to get that ribbed look!). After about 2–3 minutes the juices will start to come through to the top. When this happens turn the steak over and onto the hotplate again for 30 seconds, then back to the grill the same side up. It will take less time to cook the other side. If you want it rare, cook the second side for about 2 minutes and for well-done cook for about 4 minutes. Let the steak rest for 4–5 minutes before serving. This will allow the meat to relax and allow the juices to flow, making it sumptuous and tender.

Pork chops

Pork chops taste great when cooked on the barbeque. Loin chops are one of the best cuts to eat, as they are thick and juicy and require hardly any oil to cook. Sealing them on the hotplate before cooking is optional as they can be placed straight onto the grill, but make sure you place them in the middle – not at the back – as the pork fat will flare up and burn them if they're cooked too fast.

If you are going to seal the chops, heat the hotplate and grills on high for 10–15 minutes and then seal the chops for about 30 seconds on each side. Then transfer them to the grill, turn the grill down to low heat, and cook the chops in the middle of the grill for 6–8 minutes each side or until cooked. The chops will be quite firm to the touch when ready, like a well-done steak. These chops are great with a topping of sun-dried tomatoes for a savoury taste or apple or pineapple for sweet!

Sausages or chipolatas

Sausages are very much a part of the Aussie barbeque tradition and they are quite easy to cook, but it is important to buy a good quality raw product to begin with. The meat content of your sausages should be no less than 70% (compared to fat and other ingredients). Check the ingredients list on the packet to make sure, or ask your butcher. If the sausages you buy have a bigger meat than fat content then you will have less fat and far less flare-ups whilst cooking! One of the best things about cooking sausages on the barbeque is that you can use fresh, thawed or frozen snags, and no oil is required!

Chipolatas are baby sausages. They are about half the size of normal snags and are often much tastier. There are many varieties available, including pork, beef and chicken. Chipolatas are great to nibble on whilst you wait for the barbeque to get hot enough to cook bigger meats.

If you have a warming rack (found on most hooded barbeques), turn one burner on to high (if you have more than 4 burners turn two that are next to each other on to high), place the sausages onto the rack and close the hood. The cooking temperature should be low to medium – 150 to 180°C. Try not to place any sausages directly above the lit burner (you can place snags on top of one other if you're short of space). Cook for 15–30 minutes, turning a couple of times.

When your snags are ready take them off immediately. They will be lovely and crisp and can be served straight away or kept warm with foil.

If you don't have a warming rack or hood you can still cook great tasting snags! Turn the burners on to low on the grill side of the barbeque and place the sausages length wise onto the middle of the grill. Turn them every 2–3 minutes until cooked. If they flare up move them closer to the front, but watch them all the time.

Kebabs

There are lots of ways to make and cook kebabs. One of the easiest is to buy them already made up from your butcher or supermarket and then grill them on the barbeque, but making them yourself is also easy and lots of fun!

You will need:

2 lamb fillets	**3 capsicums (red, green and yellow for colour)**
1 thick steak (rump, fillet or porterhouse)	**Extra virgin olive oil**
1 chicken breast (or 2 thighs)	**Balsamic vinegar**
12 whole button mushrooms	**Salt & pepper**
4 tomatoes	**Teriyaki marinade**
2 onions (brown, white or red)	**Bamboo or metal skewers**

If using bamboo skewers, soak them in water for an hour beforehand to prevent them burning or catching alight on the barbeque.

Cut the lamb, steak or chicken into sizeable cubes so that they slip easily on to the kebab sticks. Cut the tomatoes and onions into quarters, top to bottom, and cut the peppers into 1 inch strips, removing the core and seeds.

Put everything into a mixing bowl and add 2 tbsp of extra virgin olive oil, 2 tsp of balsamic vinegar and 1 tbsp of teriyaki marinade. Mix together and cover the bowl with cling wrap, and store in the fridge for 1 hour.

To make the kebabs, thread the food pieces alternately onto the skewers. You can be as creative as you like, or follow the suggested order below:

Steak / onion / mushroom / chicken / tomato / yellow pepper / lamb / mushroom / green pepper / tomato / onion / steak etc.

Pack the pieces firmly but not too tight.

Light the grill and preheat on high for 10 minutes, then turn down to low. Place the kebabs on the middle of the grill, front to back so that they fit nicely into the valleys of the grill. Cook for 10–20 minutes (depending how you like them), turning regularly so that all sides get cooked.

Serve them on or off the kebab sticks with a salad or veggies of your choice.

Lamb chops

There are all sorts of chops available from your butcher or the supermarket. Loin chops or cutlets are good cuts to choose as they are smaller and have a chunk of meat to chew on at one end and a bone handle to hold onto at the other! They are a bit more expensive than the normal chump chops but well worth the extra dollar or two.

You will need:

4–6 lamb loin chops or cutlets

1 tbsp extra virgin olive oil

Salt & pepper

Light two burners under the grill and preheat on high for 5 minutes, then turn down to low. There is no need to seal these chops as they don't take long to cook and the bone keeps the flavour in.

Use a pastry brush to spread oil onto each chop, on both sides. Sprinkle on some salt and pepper. Place the chops at the back of the grill and cook on each side for 4–5 minutes. Rest them for a few minutes before serving.

Chicken thighs

Chicken thighs are a wonderful cut of meat to cook on the barbeque as they remain moist and tender. Just pull the skins off, brush with a little extra virgin olive oil and start cooking!

Light the grill and preheat on high for a few minutes, then turn down to low. Place the thighs on the middle to back part of the grill, smooth side up.

Chicken thighs will cook in 7–10 minutes on one side and 5–7 minutes on the other. They are quite hard to overcook but still keep your eye on them, just in case. They are very versatile as you can serve them with a green salad or veggies, or toss them in some fresh pasta.

Chicken breast

Although chicken breast tastes great and is very lean, it can get a bit dry when cooked on a barbeque. However, there are ways to avoid this!

Brush a little oil over the meat and cook it slowly over a low grill. Be careful not to overcook it or your meat will be dry and tough.

A foolproof way to make sure this doesn't happen is to make a ½ inch slice vertically through the thickest end of one breast fillet. When it starts to cook you will see the colour change from pink to white, moving upwards. When it gets to just under halfway, it's time to turn it over and cook the other side. When the meat has very little pink in the centre take it off and rest it for a few minutes and voila, it's done!

Chicken escalopes

Another way to cook chicken breasts is to make them into escalopes (small, thin pieces of tender meat).

To do this, wrap a chicken breast in two layers of cling wrap and using a rolling pin, gently pound the meat until it's approximately half or two-thirds the original thickness. Remove the cling wrap and brush the chicken on both sides with extra virgin olive oil. Add a sprinkle of salt and pepper. Turn the grill on high and preheat for a few minutes, then turn down to low and place the scalloped chicken in the centre. It will probably stick initially – if it does then use a spatula to ease it off – this will prevent further sticking. Cook for 4–5 minutes on one side and 3 minutes on the other. When the chicken is ready, cut it into slices and toss in a salad and serve.

You can use these escalopes as an alternative to chicken pieces in the recipe on page 86.

Chicken pieces

Chicken pieces are great to barbeque and are so easy. You can use chicken legs, wings, breasts or thighs but bear in mind that mixed chicken pieces are relatively cheap as the bones are still in and they don't have a lot of meat on them.

You will need:

6–8 chicken pieces

2 tbsp extra virgin olive oil

1 handful of fresh mixed herbs (basil, parsley & oregano, or a teaspoon of dried mixed herbs)

Salt & pepper

Mix the chicken in a bowl with the olive oil, herbs, salt and pepper. Cover and refrigerate for 1 hour.

Light the burners under the grill and preheat on high for about 5 minutes, then turn the heat down to low.

Place the pieces (bone side down where possible) onto the middle of the grill. Cook for about 10 minutes on one side and about 5 minutes on the other, until cooked. To check if the chicken is ready, slice the flesh with a sharp knife – if the knife comes out clean and the juices run clear then it's ready, if not then keep cooking! If you're not sure, take one piece off the grill and slice it open. The meat inside should be creamy with no trace of pink.

Tip: Chicken is very easy to burn so you need to watch it all the time. If it flares up, move it to the front of the barbeque where it's cooler.

Potatoes

Potatoes might be basic but they make a great addition to any barbeque lunch or dinner! Not only are they filling, they also taste wonderful with any main dish.

There are all sorts of spuds you can use – new potatoes, gourmet potatoes, red Desiree potatoes, sweet potatoes – the list goes on and on! Any potato will work in any recipe so try them all…

Jacket potatoes in foil

Lightly scrub some potatoes with water and then pat dry. To prepare each potato, cut four slits into the top using a sharp knife – two slits in one direction and then two in the opposite direction – like noughts-and-crosses. Place each potato on a 6–8 inch square of foil with the sliced side facing up. Drizzle a little olive oil onto the cuts and add a teaspoon of butter and a sprinkle of fresh or dry herbs.

Lift each corner of the foil up to the top of the spud and give it a slight twist. Don't twist too tight or it won't be able to breathe.

Place the potatoes on the warming rack of the barbeque and close the lid. If your barbeque has 4 burners or less, light the far right-hand burner only. If your barbeque has 5 burners or more, light the two right-handed burners. The hood temperature gauge should reach 180–200°C.

Cook for 45 minutes to 1 hour, until cooked through. Use a sharp knife to see if they're ready (just poke through the foil and into the potato – if the knife goes in easily then they're done).

Wrapping the potatoes in foil makes them easier to handle (you can grab them by the tops of the foil when ready), they don't stick to the foil and they look great on the serving dish – very rustic!

Serve with some sour cream and freshly chopped chives.

Sweet potatoes in foil

Peel the sweet potatoes. Take a sharp knife and cut each potato into 1 inch cubes. Take a large piece of foil and place about 10 pieces of sweet potato in the middle.

Drizzle with a little olive oil and add half a teaspoon of butter and a few freshly chopped herbs (you can use mixed dry herbs instead if you like). Then lift each corner of the foil up to the top and give it a slight twist (not too tight).

Place onto the warming rack of the barbeque and close the hood. If your barbeque has 4 burners or less, light the far right-hand burner only. If your barbeque has 5 burners or more, light the two right-handed burners. The hood temperature gauge should reach 180–200°C.

Cook for 35–50 minutes, until cooked through.

Potatoes wrapped in foil will keep warm for awhile after they come off the barbeque and can be reheated easily.

Tip: Wrapping potatoes in foil helps them cook faster.

7

Barbeque Menus

Breakfast Menu

To cook this menu you will need a hooded barbeque and a warming rack, and if possible, a side burner or wok burner.

This menu will feed 6 people. You can halve it or double it depending on your numbers.

It is really simple and easy to cook and tastes fantastic!

Eggs (choose from boiled, fried, scrambled or Eggs Benedict)

Sausages wrapped in bacon

Homemade beef burgers

Tomatoes with cheese topping

Mushrooms

Onions

Capsicums (red, green or yellow)

Muffins

Homemade bread rolls

Coffee

Orange juice

Feeds 4–6 people

Hood required

Side burner required

INGREDIENTS

For the eggs:

6 fresh eggs, at room temperature

3 muffins, halved (if making Eggs Benedict)

Butter

Canola oil spray

½ cup milk (if making scrambled eggs)

A frying pan of water and some vinegar

6 tsp Hollandaise sauce (if making Eggs Benedict)

3 rashes back bacon cut into 2 inch pieces (if making Eggs Benedict)

Paprika (if making Eggs Benedict)

Salt & pepper

For the meat dishes:

6 or more rashers back bacon

1 dozen beef chipolata sausages

For the veggies:

3 tomatoes, halved

Cheddar cheese

1–2 onions, chopped

3 capsicums (green, yellow, red), sliced

12 button mushrooms, chopped into halves

For the burger mix:

500 g fine minced beef

1 tbsp fresh herbs or 1 tsp dried herbs

½ cup fresh breadcrumbs

1 egg, beaten

1 onion, chopped

Salt & pepper

For the bread mix:

350 g bread mix flour

195 ml water

1 tsp dried yeast

1 mixing bowl (preferably stainless steel or glass)

For the beverages:

Ground coffee

12 oranges (or store-bought orange juice)

Extras:

6 slices bread (for toasting at the end)

PREPARATION

It's a good idea to do as much food preparation as you can, before you start cooking. It will prevent panic and frustration later on, and will make the cooking process easier and more enjoyable!

Bread dough

You can buy bread rolls if you don't want to go to the trouble of making them, but once you get the knack they are quite easy to make, taste great and you can add other ingredients such as sun-dried tomatoes and mixed herbs to create your own specialty rolls!

1. Place the flour in a small mixing bowl. Add the dried yeast and mix well, then add the water a little at a time, stirring until the mixture becomes dry and stops sticking to the sides.

2. Take the mixture out of the bowl and gently knead in on a flat surface for about 10 minutes, until it becomes elastic and the flour stops sticking to your fingers. Add more water if it becomes too dry or more flour if it becomes too sticky.

3. Sprinkle a bit of flour into the bottom of a stainless steel bowl and place the dough on top of it. Cover with cling wrap. Leave the bowl in a warm place for about 40 minutes to allow the dough to rise.

4. When the dough has risen, take it out of the bowl and 'knock it back' (i.e. knead it for about 30 seconds and then roll it into a sausage shape – about the thickness of a rolling pin). Then cut it with a sharp knife into nine pieces. Roll each piece into a ball.

5. Place the balls of dough into a small deep baking dish, making sure that they don't touch. Brush them with a little olive oil and then cover the dish with cling wrap. Leave them for 30–40 minutes to rise again.

They are now ready to bake!

Beef burgers

1. Mix all the ingredients together in a bowl using a wooden spoon.

2. Roll the mix up into a 3 inch (or 8 mm) thick sausage (use a little flour on your hands so the mix is easier to handle). Wrap the sausage tightly in cling wrap, and place in the fridge for about 30 minutes.

3. Remove from the fridge and with the cling wrap still on, cut the sausage into ½ inch slices (or thicker if you prefer).

Don't forget to take off the cling wrap before you cook them!

Extra preparation

Chop the onions, halve the mushroom and slice the capsicum. Store these ingredients, covered, in the fridge for the time being.

Squeeze the orange juice and keep fresh in the fridge.

COOKING

Now it's time to cook! If this is the first time you've made a big meal for more than one or two people, you might feel a little daunted. Don't worry – the following instructions will take you through each part of the menu step by step, in the exact order that you need to do things. If you are a slightly more experienced cook then you don't necessarily have to cook in this order. You can do all or part of the menu – it's your choice! The main thing is that whatever you cook, it's all ready together at the end!

First bake the bread.

Then cook the meat.

The eggs, tomatoes, capsicum and mushrooms won't take long to cook (only 3–5 minutes), so leave them until last.

Bread rolls:

Turn the burners that are under the grill part of the barbeque onto high. (Do not turn on the burners that are under the hotplate!)

Preheat the grill with the hood down, until the temperature reaches 200°C, then turn the burners down to low. Take the cling wrap off the baking dish with the bread rolls in it, and place the dish onto the hotplate. Close the hood and keep the temperature at 200°C by adjusting the grill burners to high or low as necessary. The rolls will take 15–30 minutes to cook, depending on your barbeque. When they are ready the tops should be a light golden brown. Don't worry if they take longer but be careful not to burn them!

Remove the dish from the barbeque and tips the rolls onto a wire rack to cool down. You can heat them up later if you wish. The burgers can be served in the fresh rolls.

Burgers and sausages:

Leave the burners under the grills on low and keep the hood down. The temperature should still be about 200°C (or medium). Wrap the bacon around the sausages and take the film off the burgers and place all the meat onto the warming rack under the hood (you may need to oil the rack a little to stop the food sticking). If you can't get all the food on in one go then do it in two batches, or place the burgers on top of the sausages.

The burgers and sausages should take about 20 minutes to cook. The burgers can be rare, medium or well done depending on taste and how long you cook them for. They can also be finished off on the grill to get that barbeque ribbed look! When they are done, place them in a dish and cover with foil to keep warm.

Light the burners under the hotplate and heat on high for about 5 minutes, then turn down to low. Place the capsicum, mushrooms and onions on the hotplate, add a knob of butter and toss gently for a few minutes until cooked. Put the cooked mix onto a dish and cover with foil to keep warm.

Eggs

Now for the eggs... choose your method! You can make up these eggs just before you are about to serve the breaky. This menu is designed so that you make the same type of eggs for each person, but you can always cook the eggs to order when you are a bit more experienced.

To make fried eggs:

Fried eggs are easy. You can cook them directly on the hotplate (which should still be on low heat) or on a lightly oiled frying pan on the side or wok burner. If using the hotplate, make sure it's scraped clean before you start.

Spray or brush a little canola oil onto the hotplate (or in the pan) and crack the eggs onto it one at a time, as close to the surface as possible so they don't spread too much. Also make sure the eggs are spaced well apart from each other and that the heat is kept on low. The eggs will be ready when you can touch the white bit and no runny stuff comes off onto your finger! Use a spatula to take them off the barbeque and onto dinner plates.

To make boiled eggs:

These can be done on the side or wok burner.

Light the burner and boil some water in a saucepan, then reduce to a simmer (just off the boil). Gently place the whole eggs into the pan by lowering a spoon with an egg in it (the egg should be at room temperature or else it might crack). Make sure all the eggs are covered by water (most saucepans will fit 4–5 eggs at a time). Simmer for about 2 minutes then turn the burner off and cover the pan with a lid. As a general rule, leaving the eggs in the covered pan for 5–6 minutes will produce a soft yoke, but you can leave them longer for a firm yoke. Experiment a bit and you'll get the idea!

When the eggs are ready, gently remove them from the water and place into a dish covered with a cloth napkin or tea towel to keep them warm.

To make scrambled eggs:

Scrambled eggs can be made up in a mixing bowl or a measuring jug. Crack about 6 eggs into the bowl or jug, then add ½ cup of milk, a pinch of salt and pepper and a knob of butter. (You can use cream instead of milk for a fluffier texture and richer flavour.) Mix well with a fork. Make sure the hotplate is clean and sprayed with oil. Using low heat, gently pour the mixture onto the hotplate or into an oiled frying pan on the side burner. Using a spoon or spatula, repeatedly move the mixture from the edges into the middle of the hotplate or pan. The eggs will be ready when they are still moist and look light and fluffy, but not runny. Serve in a bowl topped with a little cracked pepper.

To make Eggs Benedict (poached eggs with toppings):

These can be done on the side or wok burner. It's best to cook these eggs one or two at a time.

Before you start the eggs, fry the bacon on the hotplate then keep warm in a dish using foil. The bacon will be used at the end, when serving.

Heat some water in a frying pan until it is just about to boil, then turn down to low. The water should be about two inches deep, depending on the size of pan you are using.

Pour a splash of vinegar into the water.

Carefully crack an egg into the water, keeping the egg as close to the water as possible while you are cracking it. The idea here is to do this gently – don't plonk it in the water or it else you will break the yolk. You will know when the egg is cooked by looking at it but as a general rule it will take about 3–4 minutes. Use a large spoon with drain holes to remove the egg and place it onto a dish. Cover with foil to keep warm.

Next place the muffin halves onto the grill for about 40 seconds on each side (or until they are lightly toasted). When they are ready, place on a tray and keep warm. To serve, butter each muffin halve, place an egg on top, then a little bacon, then a teaspoon of Hollandaise sauce, and finally, a sprinkle of paprika for colour.

Tomatoes:

Finally, cut the tomatoes in half and sprinkle a little grated cheese on top. Place them on the warming rack above the hotplate and cook with the burners on low and the hood closed. They will be ready in a few minutes.

To serve:

While the tomatoes are cooking, prepare the coffee and arrange the rest of the food onto dinner plates, or place all the food on the table so that people can help themselves, buffet style.

If you find that some of the food has gone cold then you can heat it up in the barbeque (under the hood), but remember, reheating the eggs will make them hard and rubbery.

Make the toast by placing the bread close to the back of the grill, which should be on high heat. Watch the bread carefully in case it starts to burn. Thirty seconds on each side should be enough to brown.

Lunch or Dinner Menu

To cook this menu you will need a hooded barbeque with a warming rack. This menu will feed 4–6 people. You can halve it or double it depending on your numbers.

Thai chicken kebabs

Beef chipolata sausages

~~~~~~~~~~~~~~~~~~~~~~

Bolar blade roast

Roasted mixed vegetables with herbs

Rich gravy with red wine and rosemary

~~~~~~~~~~~~~~~~~~~~~~

Warm pitta bread with garlic butter

Or

Warm bread rolls

~~~~~~~~~~~~~~~~~~~~~~

Caramelised fruit

Honeyed cream

Feeds 4–6 people

Hood required

INGREDIENTS

For the chicken:

500 g chicken thighs or breast, cut into 1 inch cubes

8 bamboo or metal skewers

Thai marinade (or BBQ, soy and garlic, satay etc.)

OR

10 marinated chicken skewers from the supermarket or butcher shop

For the snags

12 beef chipolatas

For the roast:

1.5–2 kg blade beef roast

6 red Desire potatoes (other types can be used)

1 cauliflower

6 carrots, peeled

½ a pumpkin, peeled and chopped into large chunks

1 green capsicum

1 whole head of garlic

1 onion

1 cup red wine (cabernet sauvignon or shiraz)

2–3 sprigs of fresh rosemary

Rock or sea salt & pepper

Extra virgin olive oil

For the roast continued:

Balsamic vinegar

**2 tbsp fresh or 2 tsp of dry mixed herbs
(e.g. basil, rosemary, thyme, and oregano)**

Knob of butter

For the bread:

Pack of pitta bread or 6 rolls

2–3 heaped tbsp butter or margarine

3 garlic cloves, crushed

For the dessert:

825 g tin pineapple pieces

825 g tin peaches

OR

1 fresh pineapple, chopped

6 fresh peaches, peeled and stones removed

AND

2 tbsp brown sugar

1 lime or lime juice

2 tbsp honey

1 tsp cinnamon

250 ml thickened cream

PREPARATION

Nibbles (chicken skewers and chipolatas)

The nibbles can be cooked in advance just before your guests arrive. They will keep warm for about 20 minutes if covered by foil. Meanwhile the roast can be cooking in the barbeque.

Cut the sausage links so that each sausage is separate, and place on a tray, ready for cooking. There's no need to add any oil to the sausages – you can actually cook them straight from the freezer if you like!

With the chicken, there is no preparation to be done if you are using store-bought marinated chicken skewers. If, however, you are making them from scratch you will need to allow time for marinating (at least one hour).

Cut the chicken into 1 inch cubes and place in a metal bowl. Mix in the marinade, cover with cling wrap and refrigerate for at least one hour. At the same time, soak the bamboo skewers in cold water (this will prevent the bamboo from burning on the barbeque).

When the chicken is marinated, remove from the fridge and thread the pieces onto the skewers, making sure that they're not threaded on too tightly.

The roast

Finely chop one sprig of fresh rosemary and mix it in a small bowl with one tablespoon of extra virgin olive oil and add a little cracked pepper.

Spread the mixture all over the roasting meat and set aside.

Next prepare the vegetables. Slice the potatoes into wedges, slice the carrots diagonally and chop the onion into eighths. Peel and deseed the pumpkin and chop into small pieces (about 2 × 2.5 inch). Chop the cauliflower into florets. Slice the capsicum and peel the garlic cloves. Place everything into a deep bowl. Add 2 tablespoons of olive oil and some salt and pepper and mix using your (freshly washed) hands. Chop the mixed herbs and toss them through the veggies. You can use less or more herbs, depending on your personal preference.

Line a large baking dish with non-stick baking paper. The dish should not be any more than 1–2 inches deep or else the veggies will stew rather than roast. Arrange the veggie mix evenly in the dish. Add a sprinkle of rock salt, a splash of balsamic vinegar and a little drizzle of extra virgin olive oil and set aside.

Garlic butter (for the pitta bread)

In a small bowl, mix the butter or margarine with the freshly crushed garlic (you can use two teaspoons of bottled minced garlic instead if you prefer). Mix into a smooth paste and add a little salt and pepper. Refrigerate until needed.

Dessert

Whip the cream until it forms soft peaks, using a whisk, or an electric beater if you have one. Cover with cling wrap and refrigerate until needed.

COOKING

The sausages and kebabs are for your guests to nibble on while the roast and veggies are cooking. The idea of cooking the nibbles now is to not waste heat (or time) getting the barbeque up to temperature before the roast goes in!

Light two burners on the grill side of the barbeque and heat until the temperature reaches around 200°C (or medium). This will take approximately 10–15 minutes, depending on the barbeque and the weather conditions. (For example, if it's windy or cold the barbeque will take longer to heat up. If the weather is humid or hot the barbeque will heat up quicker, etc.)

Next, lift the hood and place the sausages directly on top of the warming rack, above the hotplate section so that they are not over any direct heat and any fat drips onto the plate rather than the grill.

Close the hood and keep your eye on the hood temperature gauge – don't let it get above 200°C and if it does, turn one of the burners down to low until the temperature drops. Leave the hood down for about 10 minutes.

Now lift the hood and turn the burners under the hotplate on to high. Turn the sausages so that they are evenly cooked. Don't prick them! Put the hood down and cook for a further 5 minutes.

Open the hood and place the chicken skewers onto the hotplate. Leave the hood up and cook the skewers, turning regularly, for about 5 minutes or until cooked through. By now the sausages should be nice and crisp and the chicken skewers ready to serve. If the sausages are ready earlier you can take them off and place them on a dish and cover with foil. The chicken skewers won't be far behind!

When the nibbles are done and removed from the barbeque, turn the burners under the hotplate down to low and leave only the far right burner under the grill on high. Close the hood and wait for the temperature to get back to 200°C.

Now for the roast...

The roast will take about 1–1.5 hours or 20–30 minutes per ½ kilo for a rare to medium result. Remember this is a slow-cook dish.

Scrape the hotplate of any leftover marinade and then seal the meat on all sides. Place the roast rack into the roasting dish, and place the sealed meat on the rack. The purpose of using a roast rack is to raise the meat above the roasting dish so that it won't burn.

Make sure that the barbeque temperature is just over medium, about 220°C. Place the roasting dish onto the hotplate. You may like to place another rack between the roasting dish and the hotplate. (This raises the dish higher to allow for better heat convection and reduces the chance of burning the bottom of the dish.) Remove the warming rack if it's in the way, but remember to use an oven mitt, as it will be hot!

Close the hood and cook for 30 minutes. You may need to regulate the heat by turning the burner under the grill to low or high. (Turn to low if it's too hot and high if it's too cold. If it's still not hot enough use the burners under the hotplate to regulate the temperature.)

After 30 minutes lift the hood and place the veggie tray next to the roast, halfway between the plate and the grill, if there's room. Do not place the veggie tray directly onto the grill if the burner below it is lit, or the tray will burn!

Mix the wine with a cup of water and pour it into the roasting tray so that it settles under the meat. Close the lid and cook for one hour.

The roast may take slightly longer or shorter than this to cook, depending on the cut of meat. Ambient temperatures will also affect the cooking time. The best way to check if it's done is to use a meat thermometer. Forty-five minutes into the last hour of cooking, lift the hood, turn the veggies, take the roast out and close the hood. Stick the meat thermometer halfway in, at the centre of the roast, and check the reading. If you want it rare, the temperature should be around 140°C. Medium should be around 160°C and well done should be around 170°C.

Whether you want it rare, medium or well done, you'll need to remove the meat from the barbeque before it reaches the desired temperature. On the meat thermometer, this will be one notch before the one you're aiming for. As the meat rests it will keep cooking, and will reach the desired temperature automatically (see 'Resting your meat' on the next page).

Regardless of how long you cook the meat for, you'll need to keep an eye on the veggies to make sure they don't burn. If they are ready before the meat is, take them out and place foil over them.

When all the food has been removed from the barbeque, keep the burners under the hotplate on low but turn off all other burners.

Resting your meat

You need to rest your meat before serving it. The scientific reason for this is that because the heat of the barbeque is so intense, the juices in the meat are forced up to the top as the heat rises. Resting the meat at room temperature allows the juices to flow back into the meat, making it tender and juicy. Failing to rest the meat properly will result in the meat being tough and stringy.

This roast will need to rest, covered in foil, for at least 10–15 minutes. This gives you time to make the gravy and cook the last two items before the dessert.

Pitta bread

These don't take long to cook and must be served almost immediately.

Take each piece of bread and rub the pre-prepared garlic butter on both sides, placing one piece on top of the other as you butter them.

Place one piece at a time on the hotplate for 10–15 seconds, then turn over and cook for same time on the other side. They should be light brown on each side. If not, reduce or increase the time accordingly. Place them on a cutting board, one on top of the other, and when all are cooked, cut into thirds or quarters with a sharp knife. Serve on a plate in a criss-cross strip pattern so that they can breathe and won't get soggy.

Bread rolls

Place the rolls on the warming rack and pull the hood down. Cook for about 5 minutes or so, until they are warm on the inside and crispy on the outside. You will know when they are ready! Take them off the rack and place in a wicker basket or a bowl. Cover with a clean tea towel to keep them warm until you're ready to serve.

Gravy

By now your meat should be fully rested so take it off the roasting rack and place on a carving tray, leaving the foil on. There should be some juices left in the roasting tray.

Remove the roasting rack and place the roasting tray, with the juices inside, directly on the hotplate or on the side or wok burner if you have one. Turn the burners up to high. Add a little more wine if necessary, and a knob of butter, and heat to reduce the liquid to about two thirds. Meanwhile, cut the roast into slices and pour any remaining juices into the gravy, simmering gently so that it doesn't burn. When it's done, turn all the burners off.

To serve

Place the vegetables in the centre of each plate, lay two slices of meat diagonally on top and drizzle with the gravy mix and a sprig of rosemary for decoration (this is optional). Serve immediately with the crusty bread rolls or garlic pitta bread.

Dessert

This only takes a few minutes and can be done after everyone has finished the main course.

Put the burners on under the hotplate. Pre-heat for a few minutes until it reaches medium heat, then give the hotplate a quick clean with paper towel and rub with a half of lime. The hotplate will be relatively clean, as you haven't cooked anything directly on it other than sealing the beef.

Cut the fruit into chunky slices (or open the tinned fruit, discarding the juices) and place into a bowl. Mix in the brown sugar and a squeeze of lime juice.

Pour the fruit mix directly onto the hotplate and toss lightly, caramelising the fruit, for a couple of minutes. Scoop the mix up and place into a serving bowl.

Turn the burners off.

Place the whipped cream into a bowl add the honey and cinnamon. Combine well.

Serve the fruit in individual dishes and place some of the cinnamon cream on top.

More Delicious Barbeque Recipes

Recipes in this chapter

Fish cooked in beer batter

Feeds 4–6 people

5 mins to prepare

30 mins to marinate | 10–20 mins to cook

Side burner required

Fish fillets or seafood (e.g. hoki, barramundi, groper, prawns or scallops)

500 ml canola oil

1 cup plain flour

Salt & pepper

For the batter:

½ cup self-raising flour

½ cup beer

Pinch of salt

This recipe makes enough batter for about 4–6 fillets. The recipe can be doubled if more batter is required.

To cook:

Place all batter ingredients in a large bowl and whisk by hand until it's smooth and creamy. If it gets too sticky and thick add some more beer, but not too much or it will become too runny. Cover with cling wrap and store in the fridge for about 30 minutes.

Light the side burner on the barbeque, and heat the oil over high heat in a large deep pan or wok. After 5–6 minutes test the temperature by placing the handle end of a wooden spoon into the oil. If it bubbles at the end of the handle then it's ready for you to start cooking.

Take the batter out of the fridge and give it a little whisk. Put the plain flour, seasoned with salt and pepper, into another bowl. Coat one fish fillet with the seasoned flour, holding it by the tail end, then place it into the batter so that it's well covered on both sides. Then place it gently and slowly into the hot oil, holding it for a few seconds before dropping it in to prevent the fish from sticking to the sides or to another piece of fish. Repeat with a couple more pieces but don't crowd the pan! When the fish is golden brown (you may have to turn it over a couple of times) use a small fish strainer or tongs to pick it up and place it into a wicker bowl with some paper towels in it to absorb any excess oil.

Serve immediately with lemon wedges and your favourite salad, chips or potato wedges!

BBQ prawns

20 seconds

5 minutes to cook

BBQ prawns are easy to cook and are a typical Aussie dish for the barbeque. However, many people overcook them and they become rubbery and tasteless! Cook prawns quickly for a juicy, tender result.

You can buy prawns raw or already cooked. There are many different varieties available, including banana prawns, tiger prawns and endeavour prawns. However, the king prawn is the most popular for cooking on the barbeque, as they are big and meaty and easy to handle with BBQ tongs. King prawns do come in different sizes and grades, but standard sizes are available in fish shops and supermarkets. Prawns can be bought frozen or fresh, but if you buy them frozen remember that you can't refreeze them once they've thawed.

If you don't want the mess and hassle of peeling the prawns yourself, you can buy them already peeled. They are more expensive this way but sometimes the extra cost justifies the effort of doing it yourself, especially if you need them ready in a hurry!

Prawn peelers, which de-vein and peel the prawns for you, are inexpensive and are available from kitchenware shops and department stores.

Use the hotplate to cook prawns – once heated it cooks the prawns quickly and they retain their moisture better.

To cook BBQ prawns, simply heat the hotplate for a few minutes on high, then turn the burners down to low heat and throw the prawns on. Cook them for 60–90 seconds (or 20 seconds if they've been pre-cooked), turning them two or three times, and then take them off the heat and serve immediately with lemon wedges. That's it!

Chilli king prawns

Feeds 2 people

5 mins to prepare

1.5–3 mins to cook

12 king prawns – cooked or raw (raw is better), peeled and de-veined

12 wooden cocktail sticks

3 tbsp sweet chilli sauce

1 tsp minced garlic

1 tbsp extra virgin olive oil

Salt & pepper

Half a lemon

Paper napkins

Mix the sweet chilli sauce, garlic and oil in a small bowl. Add the prawns and toss lightly with tongs so that they are well covered with the mixture.

After checking that the hotplate is clean, turn the burners under the hotplate on to full, and heat for a few minutes. Take the lemon and lightly rub the hotplate with it to get rid of any smells from the last time you cooked. Lightly spray the hotplate with canola oil and when it starts to smoke after about 5 to 10 minutes turn the burners down to low.

The prawns won't take long to cook so have your cocktail sticks and napkins ready for your guests to use. Pour the prawn and chilli mixture onto the hotplate – pre-cooked prawns will take about 20 seconds, tossed once (no more time is required as all you are doing is charring and re-heating them). Raw prawns need 60–90 seconds on the hotplate, tossed two or three times so both sides are cooked. You will notice them changing colour from translucent to white. Just before they become completely white, take them off the hotplate and place into the serving bowl. Serve immediately, using the sauce for dipping and the cocktail sticks to pick them up. Don't forget to wipe the hotplate, turn the burners and gas supply off and enjoy!

Fish fillets in foil boats

Feeds 4 people

15–20 mins to prepare

30 mins to cook

Hood required

4 fish fillets (barramundi, snapper, hake, whiting or similar)

2 red onions

2 lemons

2 tomatoes

A handful of fresh basil

Salt & pepper

¼ cup white wine

Extra virgin olive oil

4 knobs of butter

4 × 18 inch long pieces of foil

Some silicone or baking paper

Light the burners under the hotplate and pre-heat on high, with the hood open, for 10–15 minutes. While the barbeque is heating up, prepare the fish and foil boats.

Take one piece of foil and lay it flat, shiny side up. Fold ⅓ of the foil in lengthways, then fold it over again so that it's three layers thick. It should be about 18 × 4–6 inches wide, depending on the width of your foil. Lay it flat, then scrunch up about 2 inches at each end and gently twist. You can then mold the foil into a canoe-shaped boat. It should be deep enough for the fish and the other ingredients to fit easily inside it. If the boat is too narrow, just undo it and start again, folding the foil into two instead of three.

Cut a piece of silicone paper so that it fits into the bottom of the foil boat. Repeat the foil and silicone paper process until you have a boat for each fillet of fish.

Slice the tomatoes, onions and lemons. Place the lemon slices on the bottom of each boat (about 2–3 slices per boat) followed by the onion slices (about 2 slices per boat), then the tomato slices (about 3 slices per boat). The reason for using these ingredients first is that they separate the fish from the foil, which will prevent the fish from burning on the hotplate. They also help keep the fish moist and infuse flavour from the bottom up during cooking.

Drizzle a little olive oil over the top and place a knob of butter in each boat. Place the fish fillets on top of the stack and sprinkle with freshly shredded basil leaves. Finally, drizzle a little more oil and add a squeeze of lemon and some salt and cracked pepper.

By now the hotplate should be well and truly heated. Place the boats onto the hotplate and close the hood. Adjust the burners up or down to keep the temperature at around 220°C, and only use the burners under the hotplate.

Depending on the thickness of the fish, cooking time will be between 20–30 minutes. After about 10 minutes, add a tablespoon of wine to each boat, pouring it so that it settles at the bottom of the boat and not over the fish.

Check the boats every 5 minutes and adjust the heat accordingly .You will know when they are ready when they turn from opaque to white in colour and the fish falls away when you nudge it with a fork. If you're using thick pieces of fish, they are ready when you can easily push a fork through the thickest part of the fillet.

You can serve them as they are in their boats, or move them onto a plate.

Tip: You should be able to lift the fish off the hotplate by using the two ends of the boat. Use a tea towel or oven mitts as the foil ends may be a little hot.

Whole fish cooked with lemon, onion and herbs

Feeds 4 people

20 mins to prepare

1 hour to cook

Hood required

A whole fish (1.5–2.0 kg, pink or king snapper is ideal)

3 tomatoes, sliced

3 onions, sliced

3 lemons, sliced

Fresh herbs (1 sprig each of parsley, rosemary and basil)

Salt & pepper

Extra virgin olive oil

Foil

For this dish you will need a hooded BBQ and a fisharoo or fish cage.

You will need to allow plenty of time to prepare and cook the fish. It can be prepared in advance, then covered in foil and kept in the fridge.

The fish should be scaled and gutted and have the head and tail still on. If you prefer the head and tail off you can ask the fishmonger to remove them, but leaving them on adds to the presentation and flavour of the dish.

Wash the fish thoroughly and pat it dry with a tea towel or some paper towels. With the fish laying on its side on a flat surface, make several diagonal cuts into the flesh through to the bone. The cuts should be about 2 inches apart. Keeping the fish on the same side, turn it around (so the head is now facing the other way) and cut diagonally across the first cuts. Turn the fish over and make similar cuts on the other side. Be careful of the fins as they can be very sharp! There are three good reasons for cutting diagonally into the flesh before cooking:

1. You can pull the flesh off in chunks.

2. It allows the flavours from the added ingredients to get right into the fish, all the way down to the bone.

3. It takes less time to cook.

Next rub some olive oil into the flesh and then sprinkle on some salt and pepper. Do this on both sides.

Open up the fish rack and place a double layer of foil on the bottom, and then grease the foil with a little oil (spray or brush on) to prevent sticking.

Place half of the lemon slices onto the foil, then overlap with half of the onion and tomato slices. Place the herb sprigs on top.

Lay the fish over the herbs and rub some oil inside the fish cavity, then insert a few more slices of the lemon, onion and tomato into the fish cavity. Lay the remainder of the slices on the top of the fish. Add a final, generous drizzle of olive oil, then close the rack.

Light all the burners and with the hood down, watch the temperature gauge until it reaches about 200°C. Turn the burners under the hotplate down to low and leave only one burner on under the grill, on high. (Use the burner that's furthest away from the hotplate. If your barbeque has more than four burners, you may need to leave the two far right burners under the grill on.)

Place the fish cage onto the hotplate and close the hood. Watch the temperature – if it drops below 200°C turn on another burner under the grill. It's important to keep an eye on the temperature so that you don't burn the fish!

The fish will take between 40 minutes to just over an hour to cook, depending on the thickness, weight, and type of fish and the heat of your barbeque. After 30 minutes check to see how it's going. You will know when it's almost ready as the juices will turn milky and become sticky. When it's at this stage, use a knife to lift the flesh and see if it separates easily. If it doesn't, the fish needs to cook for longer. Bear in mind that the top of the fish will cook more quickly than the bottom, so check the flesh underneath if you can. The lemon, tomato and onion will keep the fish moist so don't worry if you do have to cook it for a bit longer.

> **Tip:** If you think that the top of the fish is ready but when you take it out the bottom is not quite done, remove as much flesh from the top as possible and serve it up, then place the rack back onto the hotplate. That way the top doesn't get overcooked and your guests aren't kept waiting! Check it again after about 15 minutes. It may take a while to get it completely right but it's well worth it in the end, as the fish will be moist and taste terrific!

Fish fillets in mushroom and white wine sauce

Feeds 4 people

15–20 mins to prepare

30 mins to cook

Side burner required

1 cup of white wine (chardonnay is ideal)

4 barramundi fish fillets (or similar)

2 garlic cloves, crushed

1 onion, chopped

1 tbsp unsalted butter

1 cup mushrooms, sliced

Salt & pepper

To cook this dish you will need a large frying pan. This is really a recipe for the side or wok burner, but if you don't have these extras on your barbeque you can use the grill. If using the grill, ensure that it is pre-heated for about 10 minutes before placing the pan on it.

Heat the frying pan over a low flame on the side or wok burner. Place the butter and crushed garlic in the pan, taking care not to burn the butter (keep the heat on a low setting). When the butter has melted, add the chopped onion and cook until soft. Add the white wine, then turn the heat up slightly so that the sauce simmers and reduces by about one third. Add the chopped mushrooms and a little salt and pepper to taste.

Using a spatula, move the sauce to one side of the pan, leaving some of the liquid, and place the fillets on the empty side. They won't take long to cook, so keep your eye on them.

Cook for three minutes then turn the fillets over gently with a spatula and cook the other side. Spoon some of the sauce over each fillet. When cooked, remove the pan from the heat, turn the burner off and serve the fish immediately, spooning the sauce over the top.

This dish is great for a dinner party or even a quick snack!!

Tip: With any fish, whether it's a prawn or a whole fish, make sure that it's cooked slowly and that you keep a close eye on it. Some fish are easier to cook than others, but the golden rule remains the same – low heat and constant supervision!

Grilled BBQ chicken burgers

Feeds 4 people

10 mins to prepare

15 mins to cook

4 chicken thighs, skin off

1 tbsp extra virgin olive oil

4 burger buns

1 garlic clove, crushed

4 tbsp mayonnaise

Juice of ½ lemon

2 tsp Dijon mustard (wholegrain or original)

Paprika

Salt & pepper

Put the burners under the grill onto the highest setting and leave the barbeque to warm up for a few minutes.

Mix the oil, garlic and mayonnaise together in a small bowl. Add the mustard and the lemon juice and mix thoroughly. Add salt and pepper to taste.

Using a pastry brush, dip into the mixture and lightly coat both sides of the chicken thighs.

The grill should now be ready for cooking. Slice the buns in half and place them on the grill but keep a close eye on them as they won't take long to brown! Turn them over to brown both sides then place the bottom half of each bun on your serving plate and brush with a little of the mayonnaise mix.

Turn the burners under the grill down to low. Place the chicken thighs smooth side up onto the grill and leave them to cook for 4–5 minutes. Then turn them over and cook for a further 5 minutes or until cooked through. If they flare up, move them to the front of the barbeque where it's cooler. When the chicken is ready, place them smooth side up on the bun and put a dollop of the mayonnaise mix on top. Finish with a sprinkle of paprika. Place the bun lids on the side of the chicken thighs at a 45 degree angle, so that half of the thigh is visible. This is to prevent the top of the buns getting soggy, and it also looks great!

Serve with a green salad.

Tip: Place a few bacon back rashers on grill at the same time as the chicken, but place them at the front of the grill so that they cook slowly. To serve, place the chicken on the buns first, followed by the bacon, then the mayonnaise.

Roasted chicken thighs with rosemary and bacon

Feeds 6 people

10 mins to prepare

80 mins to cook

Hood required

6 chicken thighs, skin off

6 strips of back bacon

1 tbsp rosemary leaves, chopped

2 garlic cloves, crushed

2 lemons, sliced thinly

1 tbsp lemon juice

2 tbsp extra virgin olive oil

Paprika

Salt & pepper

To cook this recipe you will need a 12 × 8 inch ovenproof dish that's at least 1 inch deep.

Before you light the barbeque, make sure the hotplate is on the left side and the grills are on the right. It's easy to swap them over if you need to.

Light the two burners under the grill and heat on high, with the hood down. Wait until the temperature reaches about 220°C, then keep the temperature steady by turning one of the burners either up or down as required.

Mix the garlic, oil, rosemary and lemon juice in a large bowl and add the chicken, coating it thoroughly.

Place the sliced lemon in the bottom of the ovenproof dish so that it's well covered.

Take a chicken thigh and place one rasher of bacon inside it, then roll it up so that the smooth side of the thigh is on the outside. Then place it, smooth side up, on top of the sliced lemons. Repeat with each chicken thigh, placing them in the dish side by side in a row. To finish, sprinkle a little salt, pepper and paprika on top.

This dish can be prepared overnight, covered with cling wrap and left in the fridge, but the paprika should only be added just before cooking.

Place a flat rack onto the hotplate and place the dish on the rack (if you don't have a flat rack you can place the dish directly onto the hotplate). Close the hood, and make sure the temperature is still around 220°C.

Cook for one hour and 20 minutes, checking after one hour to see how it's going. The good thing about this dish is that it's quite hard to overcook as the lemon keeps the chicken moist, but try to keep to the times given so that the thighs stay tender.

When ready, take the dish out, turn off the barbeque and place the chicken pieces on each plate with a lemon slice underneath and some juices spooned over the top. Serve with salad or veggies.

Tip: You can roast some veggies at the same time as the chicken (if you have room on the hotplate), then when everything is ready pile the veggies on the plate first, then put the chicken on top and spoon the juices over. It tastes sumptuous and looks great!

BBQ chilli chicken breasts

Feeds 2 people

10 mins to prepare

20 mins to cook

2 chicken breasts, skin off

1 tbsp extra virgin olive oil, plus extra for serving

2 tbsp sweet chilli sauce and a little extra for serving

2 garlic cloves, crushed (or 2 tsp minced garlic from the jar)

2 heaped tsp sour cream

Cracked pepper

Mix the sweet chilli sauce, garlic and oil in a bowl. Add the chicken breasts and mix well, then cover with cling wrap and store in the fridge for about 30 minutes. If you're really hungry then 10 minutes will do!

Spray or brush the grills with canola oil, then light two burners under the grill and pre-heat on high. After about five minutes, turn them down to low.

Take the chicken out of the fridge and place each piece onto the back of the grill, side by side. They will flare a bit initially but will settle down. Use your tongs to lift them off the grill slightly to ensure they don't stick, putting them back gently.

The chicken will take about 7–10 minutes to cook on the first side and about 4–6 minutes on the other side. As the chicken cooks, the flesh will change from pink to white. Watch the end of each piece and when it becomes white halfway through, turn them over. You will notice that the charred ribbed look will appear on the breasts as you turn them. You will know when they're ready as the meat will be firm to the touch. When they're just about ready take them off and lay them flat on a cutting board. Leave them to rest for two minutes, then spoon the rest of the sauce over them (there won't be a lot).

Using a sharp knife, cut each of the chicken breasts diagonally into ½ inch strips then gently place the strips on each plate. Drizzle a little olive oil over the top, then a little sweet chilli sauce, then a good blob of sour cream. Top with a little cracked pepper.

Serve with a green salad.

BBQ chicken thighs stuffed with bacon and sun-dried tomatoes

Feeds 4 people

10 mins to prepare

30 mins to cook

4 chicken thighs, skin off

2 large rashers back or streaky bacon, rind removed

200 g jar whole sun dried tomatoes in oil

Salt & pepper

3 kebab sticks with handles

These are simple to cook and can be served on the skewer or as individual pieces on a plate.

Place the chicken thighs into a mixing bowl, add one or two tablespoons of the sun-dried tomato oil and mix thoroughly. Take the chicken thighs out of the bowl and lay them smooth side down on a plate. Cover the top of each thigh with half a bacon rasher, then cover the bacon with a few sun-dried tomatoes. Roll up the thighs as best you can. They will be a little loose, but don't worry too much if some of the filling falls out, you can stuff it back in later. Season with some rock salt and cracked pepper.

Place the chicken pieces, smooth side up, in a row, so that they're sitting tightly together. Push one skewer through the left-hand side of all the thighs up to the end, then do the same with the right-hand side so you have two skewers holding all the meat together. Turn the whole lot upside down and thread another skewer through the middle, close to the top. Don't worry if the chicken feels a bit loose – it will tighten on cooking.

Light two of the burners under the grill and pre-heat on high, with the hood up, for 10 minutes. Then place the chicken smooth side down towards the back of the grill, with the kebab stick handles facing towards you (use a pair of gloves if the handles are metal). If the chicken flares up a bit turn the burners down to low for a while then back up to high.

Cook for 25–30 minutes, turning once after 20 minutes. Chicken thighs are very durable on the barbeque so they won't dry out easily, but cook them as slow as the grill will allow so they get cooked right through. When cooked, the chicken will be firm and moist. Take them off and either serve them on a bed of rice or with a green salad or veggies.

Apricot glazed pork leg roast (butterfly) with rosemary wine and peaches

Feeds 4 people

30 mins to prepare

120 mins to cook

Hood required

2 kg boneless pork leg roast, butterflied with crackling

½ to 1 cup white wine (Riesling is good)

½ cup water

410 g tin sliced peaches

1 tbsp fresh rosemary, chopped

½ cup apricot jam

2 tbsp extra virgin olive oil

Sea salt & pepper

You will need a hooded barbeque with a warming rack and two baking dishes (one that's big enough for the roast and another that's narrow enough to fit in the warming rack).

(Note: if you don't have a warming rack, the crackling can be cooked on a tray next to the pork, but make sure there are no burners on underneath.)

You can get your butcher to de-bone the pork for you but it's really quite easy to do it yourself.

Using a sharp knife, cut around the bone, starting with the shallow side where the bone is almost visible. Gently cut around the bone until you have removed it completely. Leave the crackling on.

Spread the pork out flat so that it's fairly even, then remove the crackling, leaving about ¼ inch of fat on the pork. Put the crackling to one side. Roughly score the meat in a criss-cross fashion on both sides, being careful not to cut too deep. Rub one tablespoon of olive oil and one teaspoon of salt all over the top of the pork, then sprinkle the rosemary on top. Season with a little cracked pepper.

Place the whole pork onto a roasting rack and place the rack into the large baking dish with some silicone paper and foil on the bottom (this is to protect the dish from mess).

Open the can of peaches and pour off the juice. Place the peaches on top of the pork. Don't worry if some fall off onto the bottom of the dish!

Rub one tablespoon of olive oil and one teaspoon of salt all over the crackling and place it skin side up into the tray (cut it into strips if it's too big to fit the in tray but try not to overlap them or they won't turn crispy).

Pour the wine and the water into a measuring jug and set aside.

Light all the burners under the grill and pre-heat on high, with the hood down, until the temperature reaches 200–220°C. Place the baking dish/rack with the roast in it onto the hotplate.

If you have a wire tray place it on the hotplate, under the baking dish, to raise the meat higher. If you haven't got one, you might like to use a regular oven rack, if it fits.

Place the dish with the crackling in it onto the warming rack above the hotplate. Throughout the cooking process, regularly take the crackling out and pour off the fat. If you leave the fat in it will get soggy and smoke up.

Close the hood. The roast and crackling need to cook initially on 200–220°C for about 30 minutes, so turn the burners down to low or turn some of them off if it gets too hot – try not to let the gauge move into the red zone!

It will take about 1.5–2 hours to cook but you will need to keep your eye on it. After about 30 minutes turn the burners down to allow the temperature to drop to 190°C. Pour the wine into the bottom of the dish, but not over the pork. Cook for a further 60 minutes then check the temperature by inserting a meat thermometer into the thickest part of the flesh. When the thermometer reading is about halfway to the pork setting (about 150°C), heat the jam in the microwave on high for 20–30 seconds or until runny, then pour it all over the pork and spread with a pastry brush or the back of a spoon. Put the dish back on the hotplate and cook for a further 30 minutes.

When the thermometer reading indicates that the roast is ready, take it off the barbeque and transfer it from the dish onto a serving plate (save the juices from the dish). Cover with foil and leave it to rest for at least 15 minutes. It should be a little charred, shiny and look delicious with the peaches and rosemary on top!

To make the sauce, pour the juices from the dish into a pan and place it on the wok or side burner on low, or on a low flame at the back of the grill with two burners on underneath. Leave it to simmer until you are ready to eat.

Slice the pork with a sharp knife and serve with the crackling, pouring the sauce over the top of the pork. There should be some peach bits in the sauce – leave them in as this adds to the look. Serve with roasted veggies.

Tandoori style BBQ chicken with yoghurt dressing

Feeds 6 people

10 mins to prepare

20 mins to cook

6 chicken thighs, skin off

2 heaped tbsp Thai red curry paste

2 tbsp extra virgin olive oil

2 tsp Thai seasoning

200 ml Greek style natural yoghurt

Keens original curry powder

Lebanese bread or flat rolls, half per person.

Salt & pepper

This is a mild curry chicken dish that is delicious and so easy to cook. Even if you're not a great curry fan, try it!

This dish should be cooked on the grill side of the barbeque. Light the burners under the grill and pre-heat on high, with the hood up, for 10–15 minutes. To prepare the chicken, place the Thai curry paste, olive oil, Thai seasoning and salt and pepper it in a glass bowl and mix thoroughly. Add the chicken and mix until the thighs are well coated. Cover the bowl and set aside.

Cut the bread in halves and place each piece on the back of the grill to brown lightly. They will only take a few minutes each side. Keep an eye on them so that they don't burn. When the bread pieces are ready, place them on a plate and set aside.

Place the chicken thighs smooth side up on the middle of the grill. If the grill is too hot turn the burners down a bit. Cook for 15–20 minutes, turning once or twice until cooked through. Thighs can take quite a bit of heat and won't dry out as much as breast fillets, so they are ideal for this recipe.

When the chicken is ready, place the bread first onto a plate then the chicken onto the bread smooth side up, then place a large blob of yoghurt on top and a sprinkle of curry powder. Serve with your favourite salad, veggies or even rice! Ideal for a snack or a main course!

Red meat

Marinated leg of lamb in honey and soy sauce

Feeds 4–6 people

20 mins to prepare

75 mins to cook

Hood required

1.5–2.0 kg leg of lamb

Honey soy marinade (buy from the supermarket or make your own – see below)

1 heaped tbsp fresh rosemary, chopped

Salt & pepper

For the marinade:

3 garlic cloves, crushed

3 tbsp honey

Pinch of salt

2 tbsp soy sauce

1 tsp brown sugar

To cook this dish you will need a baking dish and rack.

The leg of lamb can be prepared the night before and stored in the fridge to marinate. If you don't have that much time, 30 minutes to marinate is sufficient.

To make the marinade from scratch, simply place all the marinade ingredients in a bowl and mix well. You can make two batches or more if you are cooking a larger roast. Cover and place in the fridge until needed.

You can get your butcher to de-bone the lamb for you but it's really quite easy to do it yourself:

Lay the lamb leg on a flat surface. Using a very sharp knife (such as a paring knife), cut the flesh of the leg from the thinner end down towards the thick part of the leg so as to expose the bone as best as you can. As you cut, slowly and gently place your fingers between the meat and the bone, cutting against the bone as you go being very careful not to cut yourself! This will help you to make sure that you don't leave any meat on the bone.

You will end up with a reasonably flat piece of lamb. Try to keep it in one piece. If you do cut it in half that's fine – all that will happen is that you'll be cooking two bits instead of one!

The meat should end up about 2 inches thick and resemble a large steak. Do this by scouring the meat in several places on the flesh side, so that it spreads out, and lightly on the skin side so that you just break the skin. Do not cut right through it as you will end up with too many bits. Cut the shank away from the bone and keep it with the rest of the meat.

Stir the marinade well. Place the whole lamb and shank into a clear plastic bag and pour the marinade in. Massage the marinade into the meat, making sure that it gets into the scoured bits. Put the bag into the fridge for 30 minutes (or overnight).

Light the burners under the grill and pre-heat on high, with the hood closed. Don't let the temperature go higher than 200–220°C, as the meat is quite thin and will not take long to cook.

Place the rack over the baking dish. Take meat out of the bag and place it fat side up on the rack. Sprinkle over some salt and coarsely ground pepper, and the chopped rosemary.

Place the baking dish on the hotplate. Leave the two far right burners that are under the grill on high, and turn the other burners off completely.

Close the hood and cook for about an hour, making sure that the temperature does not go over 220°C. This is to prevent burning, as there is quite a lot of sugar in the marinade.

If it needs longer than an hour don't worry, just continue to cook it until the meat is tender. If you see the temperature rising, turn the far burner down to low for awhile. When cooked, place the meat on a dish with the juices poured over and rest for 10 minutes, then cut it into thick strips and serve with salad or veggies.

Hotdogs with onion and Dijon mayonnaise

Feeds 6 people

5 mins to prepare

20 mins to cook

Hood required

6 sausages (beef or pork)	**3 heaped tsp Dijon mustard**
6 hotdog rolls	**3 heaped tbsp mayonnaise**
2 red onions, sliced thinly	**Tomato sauce**
2 tbsp extra virgin olive oil	**Salt & pepper (to taste)**

Some people think of hotdogs as soggy frankfurters or snags in soggy bread – but these are different! These hotdogs are cooked the same way as you would cook chipolatas, and they taste terrific!

To make the special mayonnaise, mix the Dijon and mayonnaise in a small bowl.

Light one burner under the grill and pre-heat on high. Place the sausages in the warming rack over the hotplate and close the hood. Cook for 15–20 minutes.

Meanwhile, cut each roll through the middle but not all the way through. Prepare the onions and place the rolls and onions to one side.

Check on the sausages – if they are cooked all the way through then leave the hood open and light all the burners under the hotplate and grill and turn the heat up high. Place the rolls 'outside down' onto the rear of the grill, and watch them carefully so they don't burn. It will only take a few minutes for them to brown. Turn the rolls over and brown the inside (be careful not to split them in two). When they are all ready put them onto one large plate or individual plates. Squeeze a little tomato sauce into each roll.

Turn the burners off under the grill and take the sausages off the rack. Place them in the rolls. Toss the onions in a bowl with the olive oil, then pour them onto the hotplate and cook for a few minutes. The idea is to sear and seal them so that they are still crunchy when eaten, not soggy. When the onions are ready, turn off all the burners and put a few onions in each hotdog roll. Finish with a large blob of Dijon mayonnaise and serve immediately. Your friends will not believe how scrumptious these are until they try them!

Tip: if you find the mayonnaise mix is a bit thick, add a little lemon juice to thin it down a bit.

Ross's BBQ meatballs

Feeds 4 people
(or a party as nibbles)

10 mins to prepare

20–30 mins to cook

Hood required

500 g lean beef mince

1 ½ cups fresh breadcrumbs

½ red onion, finely chopped

1 garlic clove, crushed

1 egg beaten

1 tbsp fresh basil, chopped (or 1 tsp dried)

1 tbsp fresh oregano, chopped (or 1 tsp dried)

½ red capsicum, finely chopped

1 tsp paprika

½ tsp salt and 1tsp cracked pepper

These are great as a nibble with your sauce of choice, such as tomato, BBQ, or sweet chilli sauce and sour cream. They also taste great as part of a pasta sauce!

Thoroughly mix all ingredients (except the breadcrumbs and egg) in a glass bowl, then add the egg and about half the breadcrumbs. Mix again and then add the rest of the breadcrumbs. You should end up with a fairly firm mix.

To make the meatballs, take a spoonful of the mixture and roll it up into a 1 inch diameter ball. Repeat until all the mixture is used up. Place the meatballs on greaseproof paper on a tray and cover with cling wrap.

Refrigerate for a minimum of one hour. This will make them a lot firmer which is better for cooking.

Light two burners under the grill and pre-heat on high, with the hood closed, until the temperature reaches 200–220°C. Spray the meatballs all over with a little canola oil and place the balls in the warming rack over the grill.

Close the hood and turn the burners down to medium and cook for about 10 minutes. Then turn them over and cook with the hood down for a further 10 minutes. They should be done by now but allow a little longer if they're not cooked through. The temperature will drop a bit but this is normal, and it's better to cook them slow than to burn them!

Serve immediately on their own or with a yoghurt dip (Greek style yoghurt is the best as it's a bit thicker) or any of the suggestions on the previous page!

Vegetarian

Mini pizzas with bocconcini

 Feeds 6 people

 15 mins to prepare

 20 mins to cook

 Hood required

4–6 pieces round pitta bread

1 × 300 g tub bocconcini (available at the deli section in most supermarkets)

1 green capsicum, sliced thinly

1 red onion, sliced thinly

Extra virgin olive oil

½ cup apricot jam

For the sauce:

1 garlic clove, chopped

2 tbsp (1 sachet) tomato purée or paste

A splash of red wine

A splash of red wine vinegar

1 × 400 g can chopped tomatoes

1 tbsp tomato sauce

Salt & pepper

These pizzas are delicious and there are so many recipe varieties. You can use whatever you like as a topping, but this is a simple and quick recipe.

You can cheat on the sauce bit by just smearing some tomato paste onto the pitta bread, but the special pizza sauce is so delicious that it's worth making it if you have time. You can make a big batch of it and then freeze it for those occasions when you need it in a hurry!

To make the sauce you will need a barbeque with a side burner, or you can use the kitchen stove.

Turn the burner on to high and place a frying pan on top. Pour in the canned tomatoes. When they starts to bubble turn the burner down to low. Next add the chopped garlic, red wine, red wine vinegar, tomato sauce and salt and pepper to taste. Let the sauce simmer for 20–30 minutes or until it becomes like a paste. Keep your eye on it so that it doesn't burn, and if it's looking a bit thick just add a little water.

When it's ready, stir in the tomato paste. You should have enough for about 4–6 pizzas depending on how thick you spread it.

Light all the burners under the hotplate and grill. Keep the hotplate burners on low heat and the grill burners on high. Keep the hood open.

Heat the jam in the microwave on high for 20–30 seconds or until it's runny and bubbly. Cut the bocconcini into slices and lay out all your pizza toppings in dishes on a table.

Place the pitta bread on a flat surface and with the back of a dessert spoon, smear the pizza sauce onto the bread, then add some red onion (don't overdo it), the bocconcini (about 4–6 slices per pizza), the capsicum, then a little more onion. Using a spoon, drizzle a little apricot jam over the bocconcini, then top with a little salt and pepper and a drizzle of olive oil.

Now you're ready to cook!

Carefully place the pizzas on the hotplate and close the hood. Leave all the burners on but keep an eye on the temperature and turn off one or more grill burners if it gets over 200°C.

Cook the pizzas for 10–20 minutes. Keep your eye on them so that they don't burn. You will know when they are ready as the cheese will have melted and infused into the jam.

Take them out, cut them into triangular pizza pieces or keep them whole and give your guests some knives and forks! Serve immediately.

Tip: You may like to garnish your pizzas with a sprinkle of fresh herbs just before serving.

Potato wedges with herb seasoning

Feeds 4 people

10 mins to prepare

60 mins to cook

Hood required

1 kg washed potatoes

175 ml extra virgin olive oil

1 tsp mixed dry or 1 tbsp mixed fresh herbs, chopped (rosemary, basil, thyme, parsley, etc.)

1 tsp paprika

Salt & pepper

200 ml sour cream

Sweet chilli sauce

Light all the barbeque burners and pre-heat on high, with the roasting hood down, until the temperature reaches 200–220°C.

Having washed the potatoes thoroughly, cut them into generous sized wedges (halves, quarters etc.) and put them into a clear plastic bag. Add the herbs, then the oil, and shake the bag well to mix thoroughly and then add some freshly ground salt and pepper.

Remove the potatoes from the bag and place them skin side down into a shallow non-stick baking tray lined with baking paper. Sprinkle with paprika and place the tray on the hotplate. Close the hood and turn off the burners under the hotplate but leave the others on under the grill.

After about 30 minutes take the tray out and toss the wedges around. Return the tray to the hotplate and cook for another 15–30 minutes, depending on how crispy you want them.

Serve immediately with sweet chilli sauce and sour cream.

Tip: These are great for dips or as an accompaniment to battered fish!

Jacket potatoes in foil

Feeds 6 people

5 mins to prepare

60 mins to cook

Hood required

6 large potatoes

3 tbsp olive oil

3 tsp butter

2 tsp mixed herbs or 2 tbsp fresh herbs

200ml sour cream

Foil

This recipe is very difficult to get wrong!

Light one right-hand burner if your barbeque has four burners or less, or the two far right-hand burners if your barbeque has five burners or more. Turn the heat up to high and close the hood.

Take each potato and lightly scrub it in water and then pat it dry with a tea towel or paper towel.

Using a sharp knife, cut two slits into the potato one way and then two slits the other way (like noughts and crosses), then place it in a flat piece of foil that's big enough to generously wrap the potato. Drizzle the potato with a little olive oil, about half a teaspoon of butter and a few chopped fresh herbs (you can use mixed dry herbs if you prefer).

Lift each corner of the foil up to the top of the spud and give it a slight twist – not too tight or it won't be able to breathe. The reason for wrapping them this way is that they are easier to handle as you can grab them by the tops of the foil when ready. Also, they don't stick to the foil and they are easy to unwrap when you're ready to eat.

Place the wrapped potatoes on the warming rack of the barbeque and close the hood. The hood temperature gauge should read about 200°C or a little less.

Cook the potatoes for 45–60 minutes or until cooked through. Don't worry if it takes a bit longer. Use a sharp knife to poke through the foil to check them – if the potatoes are ready the knife should easily sink into the flesh.

The potatoes will keep warm for a quite a while after coming off the barbeque and can be reheated easily if required.

Serve with sour cream.

Sweet potatoes in foil

Feeds 6 people

10 mins to prepare

50 mins to cook

Hood required

3 large sweet potatoes, peeled

3 tbsp olive oil

3 tsp butter

2 tsp mixed herbs or 2 tbsp fresh herbs

Freshly cracked pepper

Light one right-hand burner if your barbeque has four burners or less, or the two far right-hand burners if your barbeque has five burners or more. Turn the heat up to high and close the hood.

Using a sharp knife cut each potato into about 1 inch cubes. Don't worry if some are bigger or smaller!

Take a large piece of foil and place about 10 pieces of sweet potato in the middle.

Drizzle with a little olive oil, about half a teaspoon of butter, a few chopped fresh herbs (you can use mixed dry herbs if it's easier) and a little cracked pepper. Then lift each corner of the foil up to the top and give it a slight twist – not too tight or it won't be able to breathe. Repeat until all the sweet potato pieces have been wrapped up.

By now the hood temperature gauge should read about 200°C or a little less.

Place the foil bundles in the warming rack and close the hood. Cook for 35–50 minutes, until cooked through. Don't worry if it takes a bit longer. Use a sharp knife to poke through the foil to check them – if the sweet potatoes are ready the knife should easily sink into the flesh.

The potatoes will keep warm for a quite a while after coming off the barbeque and can be reheated easily if required.

Dessert

Barbequed baked apple with cinnamon

Feeds 6 people

15 mins to prepare

60 mins to cook

Hood required

6 whole apples, skin on (any variety will do but the sweeter the better)

300ml thickened cream

6 tsp butter

6 heaped tsp brown sugar

Ground cinnamon

Foil

This is a great dessert for the barbeque, as it hardly needs any preparation and you can almost leave it to look after itself!

Firstly you will need to de-core the apples. If you haven't got a de-corer then use a small sharp knife. Simply insert the knife vertically at the top of the apple (next to where the core would be) and plunge down to the bottom. Remove the knife, then repeat on the other three sides of the core. When the core is removed you should have an apple with a square shaped hole down the middle! Make sure you remove all pips from the middle as well.

Run your knife around the middle of the apple (horizontally), making a shallow slit through the skin, and place the apple onto a piece of foil about 8 inches square. Fill approximately ⅓ of the core space with butter, sprinkle some brown sugar on the butter and then top it off with some more butter so that the butter overflows from the core space. Sprinkle with some ground cinnamon.

Crunch the foil up to the apple making sure that the top is open and the foil is quite loose. Repeat with the other apples.

You don't have to preheat the barbeque for this recipe, but obviously if it's still hot after the main course put the apples in to cook while you are serving and eating.

The best way to cook these is on the warming rack in the hood of the barbeque, over the grill side and with the burners under the grill on low. The temperature should be about 200–220°C. If it's lower than this then turn the burners up to medium or high but don't let the temperature get over 220°C. If the apples look as if they're cooking too fast then turn one of the burners off.

The apples will take between 40 minutes and an hour to cook. You will be able to tell if they are ready by inserting a knife or skewer into the top part of the apple through the skin – if it's ready then the flesh will be soft and the knife will slip easily into it.

The idea is to cook the apples right through so that the skin literally falls off the sides of the apple when it is eaten and the apple itself is soft and moist. Don't worry if the skin on the top looks a bit burnt as this can be discarded when eaten.

When the apples are ready take them out of the barbeque and serve in the foil or take them carefully out of the foil and place onto a plate. Pour the juices over and top with a dollop of cream and a sprinkle of extra cinnamon.

Bananas in brown sugar with lemon and rum

Feeds 6 people

5 mins to prepare

7 mins to cook

3 large bananas (not too ripe but nice and yellow)

Juice of 1 lemon

Brown sugar (1 ½ tsp per banana)

Rum or Grand Marnier (1 dessert spoon per banana)

Butter (½ tsp per banana)

300 ml thickened cream

Light two of the burners under the grill and pre-heat on high with the hood open. After a few minutes turn the burners down to low.

Leaving the skin on the bananas, slice them down the centre so that each banana is halved. Each half will have skin on one side and flesh on the other. Gently make some diagonal cuts about 1 cm apart in the flesh, almost but not quite down to the skin. Repeat the other way so you have diamond shape cuts.

Soften the butter and spread a little on top of the cuts, then sprinkle on a little brown sugar and then a squeeze of lemon juice.

Place the bananas skin side down onto the middle of the grill, making sure that the burners are on low heat. Cook for 3–5 minutes, depending on how hot your barbeque is.

You will know when they are almost done because you will see the sugar starting to bubble. At this stage the bananas are about two minutes away from being ready.

When they are all done, carefully remove them from the grill with tongs (they will be quite soft) and place them on individual plates or on a serving platter. Add a splash of rum or Grand Marnier and top with a dollop of fresh cream. Serve immediately!